Pencil Me In

A Trans Perspective in a Gendered World

Michael Eric Brown

Printed in the United States of America

Published by Boundless Endeavors, Inc.
2250 NW 114th Place Unit 1P, PTY 21068
Miami, FL 33179
www.boundlessendeavors.com

First Printing, 2015

Library of Congress Control Number: 2015915457
ISBN-13: 978-0-9968309-0-4 (print)
ISBN-10: 0-9968309-0-1 (print)
ISBN-13: 978-0-9968309-1-1 (e-book)
ISBN-10: 0-9968309-1-X (e-book)

Includes bibliographical references.

Dedication

To my wife, Lillian, who has been my greatest ally and joy in my journey towards living authentically, and who has given freely and unconditionally of her time, her money, and most of all her love and support to the entire transgender community.

Table of Contents

Acknowledgments i

Foreword v

Preface vii

Introduction..1

1 Being a Trans Person is not a Choice...................11

2 Mirror, Mirror – Go Away! 17

3 Missing Body Parts...23

4 Gotta Get These Things Off My Chest.................33

5 My Not-So-Mommy-Dearest 39

6 Adoption "Stories" 51

7 (Trans) Gender Primer.......................................57

8 Innocence Lost 67

9 Gendered Violence 71

10 Gatekeepers or Life Givers? 77

11 The Discrimination in Stereotyping...................89

12 Manning Up 95

13 Privilege – Not Just a Man's Subject 101

14 Being Transgender in a Gendered World 107

15 You're SUCH a Guy!...113

16 Living Authentically 119

17 Sometimes I feel like a Man... or Not.............123

18 There's Lint in my Belly Button.........................131

19 When Our Brains Are "Socially Constricted" .137

20 Do Social Circles Mean Separation? 143

21 Challenging My Position.....................................151

22 Sisters. Husband and Wife? 165

23 Society and the Realities of "Blending In".......169

24 Depression in the Transgender Population.....175

25 Self-Harm and Addiction...................................181

26 The Language of Gender.....................................191

27 Only By Seeking the Truth.................................195

Epilogue...199

Resources...201

Bibliography..205

About the Author..209

Acknowledgments

"There is no greater agony than bearing an untold story inside you." ~ Maya Angelou, *I Know Why the Caged Bird Sings*

Although in the beginning it was not my intention to write a book, over the years the thoughts and words kept flowing from my fingers to the laptop keys. Eventually, it just seemed logical to put them together in some kind of order and share them with others. I must give thanks and recognition to those who have both inspired and supported me in this journey.

My wife, Lillian, was the first person I told about the book, and from the moment she knew about it, she gave me oodles of encouragement and support right through to the end. I had been out as a transgender man for a number of years prior to meeting her, but had been unable to pursue a medical transition up to that point. When we met and I told her I was beginning my physical transition, she gave only a slight pause, then said to me, "I want to go through this with you." Those words stayed with me through not only my transition, but also through the years with my desire to offer help and support to others who were just starting out in their journeys. She continued to work full-time while I began the endeavors of online and offline support groups, founded TransMentors International, Inc., and with the eventual opening of our home as a

Trans Safe House that served the community for several years. She financially supported not only me, but dozens of people who stayed with us while starting their own transition journeys. I am deeply indebted and devoted to this awesome woman who has given so much of herself so that I can continue to educate and support my community.

To my friend and brother-of-choice Patrick, who gave his friendship to me and eventually his time and efforts to help with the Organization. He has been a faithful and sane sounding board for me when I was feeling overwhelmed as well as when I was formulating new ideas to expand the mission of supporting the trans community. Patrick is heavily involved in his own trans-related organization and serves a specific group in our community; yet he always has time to communicate, support, and encourage anyone who needs assistance. He is an exemplary model of a transgender hero who chooses to stay mostly invisible while his acts of giving and kindness serve the community in a rare and unique style. I have learned so much from him, and he has been there for me through the writing and editing of this book with his honesty and frankness regarding my written word.

To Just Evelyn, I cannot convey my sincerest appreciation of you. Your persistence in learning about transgender people when your daughter first came to you, back when transitioning youth was not yet familiar, and your subsequent work with the transgender community has surpassed even the boldest dreams of those of us who are compelled to talk to our families about our authentic selves. Your unconditional love for your daughter continues to give me and countless others with non-accepting families a hope that others will follow your example and love their trans children without reservation.

To those who came before me and alongside me – I give thanks. Some of them I have interacted with only briefly; either in person or in the digital world, while others became friends. Each have had a significant positive impact in my life (whether they knew it or not.) Some are trans, while others are allies; I won't mention all of them – but to name a few: Jamison Green, Allyson Robinson, Peterson Toscano, Helen Boyd, Becky Allison, the late Matt Kailey, Sylvia Guerrero, Kylar Broadus, Kelley Winters, Miss Major Griffin-Gracy and so many others well-known and lesser known.

Finally, to my community of trans brothers and sisters…without the opportunity you have given by your very presence on this earth, I doubt I would have been strong enough or had the courage to begin living authentically or pressed on to help others do so.

Foreword

Pencil Me In: A Trans Perspective in a Gendered World is a heart wrenching tale of human survival and a testament to perseverance that gives hope for others. In this book, Michael tells his personal story of growing up in a dysfunctional/abusive family, and his struggle with feeling good in his own body. He works through anger and self-destruction. He explores relationships with others and with society and how it relates to his perspective of himself.

There are several essays about terminology which is sometimes a contentious topic in the trans community but does not need to be as pointed out by Michael. He gives advice to beginners on the road to being more comfortable with themselves, with tips for getting ready for surgery and working with a counselor to get past some of the rough places that they will encounter. He also has topics that will challenge the more advanced within the trans community and society in general. He discusses ideas about gender and how they affect us all with or without our consent. Michael writes about a possible future where the general public will not care about which gender is present on the bus or in the bathroom. He relates an incident about his first experience in a bathroom with both men and women in line and in the stalls. That experience happened to me too, with almost the same thoughts. He infuses his essays and personal stories with great humor and insight that many can relate to in their lives.

I met Michael several years ago while visiting my trans daughter in the Phoenix area. She was very impressed with his efforts to have a home for trans people trying to get started on their own. Since she knew that having such a home was one of my dreams, she wanted me to see this organization. We visited the H.O.P.E House several times, and really liked the caring energy that we experienced with both Michael and his wife Lillian. Since then that H.O.P.E. House has closed, but there are still dreams to have such houses in other places. There is such a need for trans people to have a place to perch until they get the paperwork, counseling, and medical issues taken care of and can face the world as authentic people with good self-esteem.

Michael uses many of the ideas in the book as he advocates for and mentors others. It was an honor and privilege to meet a fellow traveler along this rocky adventurous road.

Everyone who is trans or gender questioning, or has family that is or works with these interesting people should read this book that gives such good advice and insight into our changing world.

Just Evelyn
Author of *Mom I need to be a girl*
Advocate and ally for the trans community.

San Diego, Ca.
September, 2015

Preface

Self-editing Required

"But you can only lie about who you are for so long without going crazy." ~ Ellen Wittlinger, *Parrotfish*

Why did I choose to name this book "Pencil Me In"? I'll tell you...

Many people upon meeting me and discovering that I am a Transman ask me who I am and ask me to share more with them about myself. For a very long time I found the answer difficult to share. Oh, there are a lot of words to describe the type of person I am, to explain why I do the things I do like share my own personal experience of being a trans person and share my knowledge and limited wisdom, what my profession was, or where I've lived and other personal experiences.

But does what I say about me *really* describe who I am? I don't think it does. So who am I, really? I ponder, and am introspective. I reach into the depths of my Being; I push past fears and insecurities. I poke around in the dark corners and forcefully attempt to pull out the lingering pieces of baggage and toss them into the light where I can evaluate their weight and necessity. I find it's time to replace those old bags, so I throw them out. *When I look back inside, what do I see?*

I laugh. I cry. I feel pain, I feel happiness. I hope

and I dream. I see injustice and bigotry, and I choose to respond with love. I step up from the momentary thoughts and feelings of negativity, choosing peace – rather than contention – within myself. I look around me to nature, to science, to medicine, to a Higher Power, to humanity; and, I choose to accept the Gift of Life. I see other's struggles, I empathize with their pain, and I offer my heart to them in hopes they can see past the temporal distress and know there is *good* in life.

In this feeble and fumbling attempt to explain the complexities and the simplicities of me, I realize that I am ever-changing, and there is no one word or one phrase that can simply answer the question of who I am. I choose to believe there is no permanence in life, much like being penciled in with the eraser nearby, with innumerable edits to define me. In defining *me*, I'm able to see more clearly who others are. I'm able to look within in order to begin looking outwards, and I start to see others with their own struggles and triumphs, In doing so, I'm able to see all of Life's edits – the attempts, the successes, the rejoicing and the sorrows – all sketching the foundations of who we are and who we'll become.

I'm not alone, nor have I ever been, in my journey to finding myself. I've encountered the struggles of being differently gendered in this gendered world, much the same as most other trans men and women have also. It is my hope that in sharing my perspectives in this book that I might reach others to let them know they, too, are not alone and others do understand, and as well reach the wider community of society's open-minded individuals who are seeking to find answers regarding their loved one's gender journeys.

Introduction

"Trauma or no, I would have been trans no matter what body I'd been born with. Tell the doctors that we exist for the health of humanity, which needs to find wholeness and belief in complexity. Girl in boy's body or boy inside a girl; call it fate or biology, will, or spiritual choice. But I was not born in the wrong body." ~ Scott Turner Schofield, *Two Truths and a Lie: A Memoir*

RANDOM THOUGHTS swim through my half-consciousness this morning as I sit in front of the laptop with my overly-sweetened cup of coffee. The air has crispness to it being one of the last days of comfortable coolness before the heat of the sun takes over for the next few months. I suppose I should introduce myself and tell you a bit about me; who I am. What I am. And most importantly, why I am.

My name is Michael Eric Brown. My name is special to me. It's not the one I was given at birth. In fact, my name on my original birth certificate was "Baby Girl", because I was not given a name when I was immediately put up for adoption. The name my adoptive parents chose was "fitting" for a girl name, but it was one I fought from the earliest times I remember. I changed my name a few times through the years, each time thinking, I believe on some subconscious level, that a new name would help me find myself. It wasn't until a time in my life where I actually did find myself that I was able to choose this name I will have for the rest of my life.

People describe me in various ways from "thoughtful" and "quiet", to "fair" and "tireless", to a "tell-it-like-it-is" kind of guy. People either love me or hate me as the old saying goes. Anyone who knows me knows I rarely become publicly involved in controversial discussions; therefore, very few know how I really feel and what I really think about many things that happen in the world, as well as around me, personally. Yes, I'm guarded and careful, because I understand the power of words, how words affect perceptions, and how perceptions affect attitudes and beliefs.

Some people ask me how I became involved with the transgender community, what possibly brought me to a life of service helping them. Many of these people look at me and have no idea that I'm a transman. When I tell them my story, they are visibly surprised, even shocked.

I tell them I'm a transman, and that I've experienced discrimination, and that I was homeless for months. I tell them that I had suffered severe depression and suicidal thoughts for several years, until I came to a point in my life where I realized the need for transition. Without fail, their response is not what I think it should be, for instance, "Oh, I am so sorry to hear this happened to you" but instead, it's "You were REALLY born a girl?"

Sadly, they usually never hear the point of my story. They are too busy exclaiming "Wow, I would've NEVER known – you look so….so…." and they stutter, and I think to myself, I look so… what? … "Normal?" "Real?" Sure enough, something along those lines comes out of their mouth. Find an adjective and tack it on to the end of their surprised exclamation, and that's the sum total of me in their eyes.

The questions follow, "When did you decide to become a man?" (*and I feel the need to explain that I've always been a man, I didn't just wake up one day and "decide to become a man."*) They go on… "Do you have a, you know, a.. a…'penis' now?" (*Them whispering the word "penis" like, it's a bad thing?*) to which I reply, "I'll answer that question with a question for you. Do you have a vagina?" if it's a female, or if it's a male, I ask, "Do you have a penis?" They stutter again, they stammer, sometimes they blush, and they look at me with a priceless expression. I then proceed to explain why that is an inappropriate question to ask not only a transgender person, but anyone; and I ask them how it made them feel when I asked them about their genitals. Point taken.

As early as I can remember, I used to put my dad's clothes on. I loved the way they smelled, and the way they felt on me. Even when they were just draping over me and dragging on the floor, they still felt "right." As I got older into my young teens, I especially liked his old army fatigues and his white t-shirts. My dad was a small guy, so except for the length of his legs, and the size of my butt and hips, I was able to fit his clothing fairly nicely. Well, the boobs got in the way of course, but it didn't matter as long as I was able to button the shirts.

When I left home at eighteen, it was in a hurry after a fight with my mother. I made sure as I was leaving that I got away with the couple of pairs of army pants and shirts and, of course, his T-shirts. I proudly wore these items of clothing amongst the staring and the ridicule from those in my small hometown. It did not matter to me, because I was just *being me*.

I remember wishing I could wear them all the time, and when in clothing stores I could not avoid perusing the men's section. I used to watch men around me; looking at their beards, mustaches, and arm and leg hair, and all the while wishing it were mine. I had already stopped shaving my under arms and legs in high school, much to the dismay of all those around me. You can imagine how that looked, but I didn't care.

I began searching for others like myself. I didn't even know how to find them. I assumed it would be with the "lesbians" I had been warned about. When I found them, I found other women who also did not shave. I felt at home with these others, but not as a lesbian, though I didn't know what else to call myself at the time. I went with it because it gave me "permission" to dress how I wanted to dress, and I was accepted in this community.

I began attending a local MCC church soon after finding the community (I suppose because religion had been so deeply instilled into me.) One weekend, we went on a retreat to a bigger city several hours away, and we all stayed in a hotel. We shared rooms, and in my room were three gay men and myself to share two beds. I felt like the luckiest person in the world, especially when I found who I was going to sleep next to that night.

I got undressed down to my underwear and T-shirt, while my sleeping partner stripped right down to his shorts. I was thrilled to see that he was covered in hair from head to toe, and front to back. Once we were in bed, his back to me, I ignored any reservations I was feeling and asked him if I could touch his hair. He chuckled and said yes, and quickly my hands were all over his back feeling the "rug" of hair that covered it. It was exciting, but it was also making me sad. Sad, because I knew I could never have hair like that. It didn't stop me from daydreaming though, and in my mind the way I chose to see myself was a furry little bear.

Many, many years later and thanks to Testosterone, I have become the little bear I always wanted to be, with the exception that I don't have "rug" of hair. But I do have hair on nearly all of my body. My butt and hips have disappeared and, well...wearing men's clothes and shopping in the men's departments as a man (rather than a butch-looking woman?) HELL YES!

Dreams can and do come true. I have found out that dreams aren't always full of roses, however; one still has to deal with a few "thorns' now and again. Gender is a vast subject defining all that we do, hear, see and say.

I chose to publish this book because it is just one way I can share with those in the transgender community as well as society as a whole just what being transgender is all about. I am already known publicly as a transgender man, but many who know me don't know my story.

I fully understand why many people in the transgender community choose to live quietly after transitioning. There's a lot of time, work, and explanations involved in being "out" as a transgender person. It's so much easier to just go through the remainder of your life with only your partner and maybe a few select friends knowing your "secret," than to have to face questions, and stares, and discrimination, or even violence.

I believe the governments, the politicians, and the media along with all of the activists out there fighting for our right to exist comfortably, without discrimination, and for our right to experience equality in all areas, are absolutely necessary and have made great progress in our society. I believe they must continue for as long as it takes for these things to happen. It is happening already, and will continue.

However, I can't imagine hiding who I am or where I've been; and to me, education on a face-to-face personal level is the only way in which I can foresee a widespread change in society's attitudes about transgender people. The laws may change, but until the very people responsible for upholding those laws – whether law enforcement, medical personnel or even our employers and landlords – have their minds and hearts touched by us on a personal human level, we will continue to experience the discrimination. Additionally, I feel a need to support those who have experienced the discrimination in any way I physically, emotionally and financially can. This is why I do what I do – with service to the transgender community.

I can say without giving away the rest of the book that being a transgender man is not always easy, and for me, my life really only began when I accepted who I am. Prior to this acknowledgment, my life was full of anger, fears, and deep-seated depression. If I had not chosen to live my life authentically as the man I am, I doubt I would be alive to share my story. I still encounter situations and people that challenge the person I am, but I always remember where I've been and where so many others have been and are currently so that I can find ways to approach these challenges to effect positive change in our world.

This book is written for the trans community and our allies, as well as for the wider audience of society in general. I use the terms "trans" and "transgender" throughout this book, with an occasional reference to the term "transsexual". Chapter 7 explains my thoughts on these terms, but to sum it up as a preface I want to clarify that when I use any of these terms, it is for ease of writing – *not to be exclusive to any individual's preference of identity.* Not everyone identifies as transgender; some prefer the term transsexual while others simply refer to themselves as man, or woman, or gender variant or gender-fluid (and so on). I will abbreviate and use the term "trans" occasionally, and I ask you to accept it for the wider audience I am attempting to reach. Again, as noted in the book's subtitle, it's really just a matter of perspective.

I do want to say that these writings are a collection of my thoughts, online blogs, and notes I've written over the last few years, as well as my ramblings on gender – roles, stereotypes and more. I have tried to keep the writing as reader-friendly as possible, and I have limited any academic or professional references as much as I could because I don't want it to sound in any fashion like a textbook. It is simply a compilation of personal stories along with opinions, observations and evidence of the subjects I have covered. There is a bibliography at the end for those who are interested.

Let me repeat – these thoughts are mine. Whether you agree with them or not, whether you believe I'm full of something or whether you believe I'm spot-on; they are mine. I own them.

You may laugh, you may get irritated, or even angry at what you read. You may have similar experiences, or you've experienced nothing even remotely similar. There's no specific structure to these writings, because thoughts don't happen that way. At least, my thoughts don't. They just happen, and when they do, I write. I've tried to keep a somewhat linear pattern to the chapters, but you'll find a few zigzags here and there. That's just how it happens to be.

If anything I have written helps you in any way, I'd like to know about it. If not, I'd like to know what you were expecting, or what I left out that could have been more relevant to your own expectations when you picked this book up to read it. You can always find me or my writings somewhere online in one of my blogs, social media accounts or at any one of the major book retailer websites.

Enjoy. Or not. The choice is up to you.
Michael Eric Brown, 2015

1

Being a Trans Person is not a Choice

"Being a transsexual is not something we do in the privacy of our own bedrooms; it affects every aspect of our lives, from our driver's licenses to our work histories, from our birth certificates to our school transcripts to our parents' wills, and every relationship represented by those paper trails." ~ Jamison Green, *Becoming a Visible Man*

I CAN'T COUNT the number of times I've been asked "Why (or when) did you *decide* to become a man?" In the beginning, I felt angry when someone asked this, but I've since realized that they are generally asking because they have a need to understand... they are asking for education. Turning my initial anger into seeing the opportunities, and giving a positive response has helped enlighten the minds and hearts of many.

I did not *decide* to become a man. Being a transgender person is not something that occurs when you wake up one day and think "Gee, I'm tired of being a girl, I want to be a boy from now on." One cannot "become" a transman or a transwoman; one is born as a trans person, whether they realize it or not at an early age or whether they have reached the age of retirement. Somewhere in the whole scheme of genetics and biology, a female-bodied person comes out of the womb, but in all other aspects, that person is male. The same goes with a male-bodied person, who knows at some point in their life within their heart, soul and mind that they are not what their bodies are reflecting.

Some people are born as Intersex, with perhaps extra chromosomes, or commonly enough, with both male and female sex organs; either internal or external, or a mixture of both. More often than not, the "choice" of which gender role this child will live is made by the parents or the doctor who, in many instances, make the "wrong" choice. The child is raised in the gender role forced upon him or her, sometimes to the extent of having "corrective" surgeries to reinforce this choice. When the child comes to an age of thinking on their own, many times the forced gender role is not their true gender identity.

The term "transgender" simply means someone does not fully identify with the gender they were assigned with at birth. I was born in a female body, but have never thought of myself (identified as) a "female." Yes, I lived in a female "role" (and I'll discuss more of roles throughout the book,) because that's what I was expected to do. But it wasn't without its consequences.

As a young "girl", I fought wearing dresses, and I hated purses, and gloves, and patent leather shoes. As I got older, I became shy and embarrassed about my body, and tried to hide it by wearing clothing that came up to my chin and down past my ankles and wrists. I couldn't look in a mirror, (ever, for years,) because that person looking back at me was NOT me. It was seeing a strange "ugly" person who I didn't know. I couldn't explain what the problem was, when I didn't understand it myself. I just knew I wasn't "right", I was "different", and I did not, and would not, conform to the demands which my parents, the schools, the church and others pressed upon me without some major temper tantrums erupting from deep within my being. Insulted, demeaned, and punished for my non-conformity, an anger began to grow inside me, one that followed me through much of my adulthood.

In my early childhood, screaming and demanding paid off occasionally. I was allowed to play with G.I. Joes, although they still gave me Barbie dolls. I had Tonka Toys, and race cars, but also was given dollhouses and ballerina lessons. I had the patent leather shoes to go with my pretty Easter dress and bonnet, but was occasionally allowed to wear my dad's T-shirts and army jackets when I was home and not going out anywhere.

I made up a name for myself early on – a boy's name – because I couldn't relate to the female name I was given. When my younger sister and I played together, we morphed into "John and Julie". Julie was not her real name, but the actual name of our "game" and the part she played in it. I was John. The Man, the Protector, the Strength, the Husband. I "took care of" Julie, my wife, my fair maiden. We went on our imaginary journeys across the oceans and escaped into our world of fantasy. I put on my dad's clothes, she put on my mom's dresses and shoes, and we faced the challenges of our lives as the "married' couple we imagined we were. In my own mind, it was fact; and I felt alive, and real, and lived for those precious moments of time with my sister, my "wife". I'll talk more about this in a later chapter.

Eventually outgrowing this phase of our lives, I went on to live the next part of my life in a non-typical "female" sort of way. I continued to fight my parents for the right to wear what was comfortable, but the only times I would win was when I wasn't leaving the house. Shortly after I graduated high school and had left home two weeks later, I tried first the marriage thing – to a young man I had dated for the previous three years. That didn't last long at all, and within a few short months I was certain being a housewife was not the life I had envisioned for myself.

I realized early on that I was bisexual, (which, of course, didn't fit into the whole heterosexual marriage thing,) but in order to enjoy women, I found I had been given a label. I needed to "identify" as a lesbian, as the term "bisexual" wasn't yet a popular or as widely used in society then. Or at least, this was all according to the community I found during my short marriage, the LGBT community (although back then, we were all just "gay and lesbian." The B and the T and the Q and all of the other letters hadn't been comfortably tacked on yet.) I lived in a few "lesbian" relationships over the years, but I was never comfortable with others labeling me "lesbian." Not to mention that being a "lesbian" somehow didn't compute with my bisexuality.

I was not a lesbian. I knew that. I did not relate in any way, shape or form to the other lesbians I knew, with the exception that I did enjoy other women. I was often told through the years (usually in anger or disgust) that I sounded like and thought like a man. Inside, I jumped for joy, (because I KNEW I wasn't a girl, but it hadn't "clicked" yet), but something was dreadfully wrong on the outside (and obviously inside, too.) Somehow my own sense of identity, which I later learned was my gender identity, and my sexual orientation were lumped together, and I was simply unable to see or understand the difference between the two.

It wasn't until many years later, (even for some time after I claimed the identity of male,) that I heard the term "transgender". I had known about transsexuals, but always believed it was for male-to-female people. It just didn't occur to me that a female-bodied person could transition into a male-bodied person. Looking into it and researching deeper to find out more about transgender people and transsexual people, I realized with an overwhelming sense of awe, excitement, peace, joy and happiness that this was my "problem" and it could be "fixed." I was simply born with the wrong anatomy. With the help of science and medicine, I could become outwardly the man I had always been within. And if I had to label myself (for the sake of others) I could be "trans" or "transgender" or "transsexual". But labels didn't and don't matter to me personally, though they seem to still be an issue, or perhaps a need, for many around me.

I can look in the mirror now (too often, I've been told,) and really *see* myself; I can smile, and laugh, and be proud of the person I am. There is no longer anger, there's no sadness, loneliness, or despair. There is simply the knowledge and the peace that I am a valid human being. My body has been aligned with my mind, and for that, I am grateful.

Being a transgender person is not a choice. "Transitioning" physically into one's true affirmed gender *is* a choice. There's a huge difference. One left to another chapter or even another book, or better yet, one left for others to cover the difference. Some have already done so in books, blogs, videos and writings across the Internet. Do an Internet search of the terms, you'll find them.

2

Mirror, Mirror – Go Away!

"Sometimes, I really can't believe my journey. I woke up this morning and went to the bathroom and DID NOT avert my eyes as I passed the mirror. I realized that ever present, lifelong pain that ached deep down in my core, is now gone. Completely gone. Today I feel comfortable in my own skin. It changes everything. I think I'm relating to other people better, and it's much easier for me to be kind. I'm so grateful I stuck around and finally found the courage to transition. It has been worth it."
~ *Trystan Marl Greist*

IN THE FIRST CHAPTER, I spoke of not being able to look in a mirror for many years. I realize now that it was more than just gender dysphoria that prevented me from seeing my own reflection, although seeing an average female-bodied person looking back at me was definitely disconcerting and much more than just disappointing. My mother is to blame for the other reasons, and I will share things about this part of my life and about her, because I believe there are many out there who have suffered similar abuses, and I want you to know you aren't alone, and there is healing from these abuses.

I do want to preface with this…that although there was abuse growing up, I believe there were also some good things. I had piano and oboe lessons, and I learned music appreciation. For a short while, we had ponies and my sister and I learned to ride and take care of them, and we had chickens, dogs and a cat. We were active in various 4-H subjects for many years (my mother, of course, was the Leader,) and we both learned to cook, and sew, and take care of many of the basic necessities in life. We both went to private schools, although they were very conservative "Christian" schools. One "punishment" that was prevalent for my sister and I growing up was to memorize an entire dictionary page of words with their definitions. Although we struggled and hated this, we did learn a good command of the English language, and for that I am grateful.

My mother fixed my hair and dressed me until I was twelve years old. Yes, she was weird. My hair was naturally curly, so there wasn't much that could be done. She either made my clothes or shopped at local thrift stores, so I was never wearing anything like the other kids at school. Many of my clothes were pink, as were my bedroom decorations – bedspread, lamps, and rugs. I was still stuck with the clothes she provided to me until the day I left home, never having any clothing that was popular or current, and pink was often the prevailing color. I hated pink. Pink represented "female" and I absolutely wanted nothing to do with it.

All in all, although there was a lot of not-so-good growing up, there was enough good to help prevent both my sister and I from becoming entirely crazy and institutionalized for life.

As I will mention later this book, from the time I was little until the time I left home, my mother was constantly finding something "wrong" with me, and taking me to doctors to "fix" me. Before grade school, it was "She's pigeon-toed," so I wore braces on my feet and legs to help this. By late grade school or early junior high, "Her spine is curved too much." You guessed it, a back brace to keep it straight. I was constantly told that my arms were "too short," and that I was overweight *"When I was ten years older than you I weighed less than you do and you're only 14."* Not that being adopted made a difference to her, we had entirely different body types and bone structures, and by the time I'd reached my full height of 5'3", I was nearly three inches taller than her.

Then there was my near-sightedness – glasses weren't good enough, so six years of monthly trips for years to the eye doctor an hour and a half away for contact lenses that "corrected" my vision (it did to a certain extent, but I'm still very nearsighted, and don't believe I would put anyone through what she did to me for such a small result.) And, don't overlook the four and a half years of braces, (my teeth were really not that crooked, but she insisted.) My toes were too little, my fingers were stubby, my pubic hairs were too thick (what was she doing looking, anyway?) and nearly two years of dermatology treatments for acne. Along with all of this came the drugs and doctors to "fix" my behavior for the six years before leaving home for good. In those last six years of living at home, I don't believe a week went by when I wasn't at some sort of "doctor". It wasn't until many years later that I realized I had been an innocent victim of Munchausen's by Proxy. I'll get to this more in depth in a later chapter.

Back to the subject of this chapter...I don't recall looking in a mirror before I was twelve or thirteen years old. I didn't have to because my mother made sure I presented the way she wanted me to look. And...I was ashamed. I am sure I did not want to see the little dress-up doll she made me into. The first time I remember really looking in the mirror, it was with a feeling of horror and shame. I recoiled with what and who I saw in that mirror. Inside, I had always tried to see myself as a boy, a younger version of my dad. I envisioned blond hair (nope, not happening,) blue eyes (I do have blue eyes,) and a young buff body (hardly). I had a poster on my wall of Vincent Van Patten when he was a teen in the early Seventies, and I prayed every night that I would wake up and look like him. I know you're not surprised that it didn't happen, but to me it was disturbing.

I spent the next good part of my adult life not looking in the mirror unless I absolutely had to do so. I had no mirrors in my home except for the inevitable bathroom mirror. I absolutely hated what I saw. I was thankful I had curly hair, since not much went wrong with it as long as I kept it cut short enough, so I didn't have to look to see if it was acceptable. I nearly always lived with someone, so I didn't have to look in a mirror to make sure my clothing was acceptable, I just had to ask them if I wasn't sure.

Once I transitioned and met other transgender men, I found that I wasn't alone in my avoidance of mirrors. However, by the time the Testosterone began taking effect, mirrors quickly became my friend. As new hairs grew in on my face, I was at the mirror inspecting each one. I had already cut my hair to a very short buzz cut a few years earlier and, once the hair on my temples began to recede, I rejoiced looking in the mirror. The acne now was a gift – because it meant the stuff was really working! My body began to go through changes – my buttocks and hips disappeared to nothingness, and I was thrilled to look in the mirror over and over to see all this happen.

My body is proportionate enough, despite what my mother led me to believe. I'm short, have a beer belly (and I don't drink beer!) and can grow my beard and mustache as long or as short as I want them to be. It's okay with society that I don't shave my legs and underarms, unlike it was all of those years living in a female role and not shaving. I am comfortable with who I am now. I like how I look, and do occasionally wear pink without it adversely affecting my sense of identity. I can look in the mirror and smile, and see myself smiling back. And that is priceless to me.

Like I said, my story of mirrors isn't unusual. I have talked with many transmen and transwomen, and nearly all have agreed that looking in the mirror prior to transition was not the highlight of their day. Most of them avoided mirrors for the same reason – their true selves weren't the reflection looking back at them. I don't have a lot of advice on how to get through it, but I will talk about it more in the next chapter.

3

Missing Body Parts

"It is an awful thing to be betrayed by your body. And it's lonely, because you feel you can't talk about it. You feel it's something between you and the body. You feel it's a battle you will never win . . . and yet you fight it day after day, and it wears you down. Even if you try to ignore it, the energy it takes to ignore it will exhaust you." ~ David Levithan, *Every Day*

FOR AS LONG as I can remember, I've had a penis. Well, at least in my head I do. Because of my grandfather's abuse, I learned about penises when I was very young. I was about three or four years old when I walked into my parent's bedroom one morning and reached into my dad's pajamas and pulled out his penis. I don't recall doing this, but I was told about it when I was older. I'm not sure why I did it but I imagine it's because it was what I was forced to do with my grandfather, so I didn't know I shouldn't be doing it with my dad.

I finally figured out by the time I was in second grade that all boys had penises, and girls did not have them, (although I still believed I had one, it just wasn't growing very fast.) I wanted to play with the boys, but I wasn't accepted in their games. Then one day, a young, blond, blue-eyed eight year old dream-of-a-boy came up to me and asked me if we could play "house" together. I was only eight years old too, but I was thrilled. I thought he was perfect for me. I told him to call me "John" which he did with a bit of reservation, but what did we know at that age about gender roles and conventions? I thought that since we were sharing our make-believe house together (which was really just a spot of lawn beneath an enormous fir tree) that we should make it official, so I asked him to kiss me. He finally did after I bribed him with a dime. Looking back, I laugh at that – paying a boy to kiss me – but when I stop to think about it, I have to remember that I was only in second grade and being abused by an adult, so I was unaware that sex was something one should wait for until they're older.

Throughout my grade school years of being "John" the Protector as my sister and I played together reinforced my belief that I had a penis. My thoughts were as follows: I was the husband. Husbands are men. Men have penises. Therefore, I had the right equipment, and I was a man. By the time I was eleven or twelve I was ready for sexual exploration with my sister. She was open to the idea when I told her that it was part of being "married," but then, she was only nine years old. When we actually got down to trying something, however, I discovered there was no easy way to do it, because I didn't have a penis. I was emotionally destroyed. Not long after the incident, our game of John and Julie was ended for good and I resigned myself to the fact that I was a girl, and then continued with my life living in that role for many years. I never gave up imagining my penis, though. I think I may have thought, for a while at least, it was just stuck somewhere up inside me and hadn't come out yet.

I don't believe I'm alone in my fantasies. I believe most transgender people have yearned for the body parts they weren't born with. I have spoken with countless transmen who dream of having a penis, and as many transwomen who envision having a vagina. There are those, of course, who are perfectly happy with the parts they were born with and this, as well as the former, are common in the transgender community.

For some, a surgery is out of reach due to costs. Many insurance companies, as well as the federal government, are coming around now and are finally including gender reassignment surgeries in their list of benefits. Considering the high rate of unemployment for transgender people, however, the costs are still prohibitive. Hormones can do wonders for both men and women, but even the co-pays are too much for some.

The technical term for the discomfort or distress one feels when there is a mismatch between a person's biological sex and their gender identity is Gender Dysphoria. This is a recognized medical condition, *not a mental illness or a disorder*. People who experience this dysphoria are generally considered transgender, or transsexual. Prior to transition, even prior to knowing what to call those disturbing feelings when one has been born into a body that doesn't match one's brain, the confusion and anxiety eventually consume one's life.

During my time working within and for the transgender community, I've heard countless people talk negatively about their pre-medically transitioned bodies. One fourteen year old wrote, "I'm really struggling with my body. I hate that I don't have a dick, and that people see me as girl," while another in their twenties wrote "I have felt that there was something missing since I was about three years old."

Most transgender people just starting out in their journeys have a negative self-image, mainly because they are acutely aware that their physical body doesn't match their gender identity. I can empathize with them, having come from a similar experience. Although it took me a long time to accept it for myself, I can only try to relay to them "Your body isn't who you are."

So now I say, first and foremost – I don't care if you are tall or short, overweight or the proverbial toothpick, black, white, purple, have a penis, have a vagina, blue hair, tattooed, have a physical impairment, have six-pack abs, are transgender or not transgender – YOU ARE NOT YOUR BODY.

Body image. Okay, there. I said it. The two words put together that stir up all kinds of images and emotions in nearly every human being. For many, the emotions are of the negative kind – shame, disgust, even anger. The media perpetuates what they tout to be the "perfect" bodies for men and women. Not an advertisement, billboard, news anchor or television show goes by without portraying images which reinforce what is acceptable and what is not.

Negative body image isn't unique to the transgender community. In fact, it's a national epidemic. One organization's website shares that perceptions of male body image have continued to increase over the last thirty years from 15% to 43% of men who aren't happy with their bodies, as well as 20 million women and 10 million men suffer from an eating disorder at some point in their life (National Eating Disorders Association). Body image, and mentally coping with what we look like to ourselves, is something that everyone struggles with from time to time. Media reinforces that only a select few actually meet the standards of "body perfection". After they've added a bit of Photoshop here and there, we find there is no way that anyone, anywhere, could ever live up to these hyper-idealized appearances.

For many transgender people, it is a life-long struggle between the inner sense of self and the physical self – the external part of self that is tangible and the part that presents itself to social and cultural scrutinizing. It's a struggle between expressing and repressing one's true self in order to be accepted or belong in relationships and society. The fear of rejection is *directly related* to the psychological distress of a negative body image. As a child, there is no incongruence or body dysphoria until confronted with the socially acceptable image society has placed upon their sex. Once this happens there is shame, disgust, ridicule and discouragement from presenting as their true gender.

I don't know that there's an easy answer for those who live with negative self-image because of their body. I can say what the experts tell us – learn to accept the body we have and stop comparing ourselves to other people – but I know for transgender people, this doesn't help. Our bodies are purely genetically formed, it's not a matter of going on a diet to lose weight or exercising to build up some muscle. I know we can't just look in the mirror and say "Gosh, I really need to lose some weight, I'll start eating better and get a gym membership to get in shape." We have extra body parts or missing body parts that are a giveaway to the rest of the world that we are either chromosomally XX or XY and there's not much we can do about it. We can bind and tuck and shave and wear clothing that matches our affirmed gender. We can take hormones and, if we're fortunate enough to have a way to pay for it, we can have surgeries.

The things I can tell you that might make it a bit easier when you're going through a tough time with your self-image may help a little, so give them a try.

First, remove yourself from people who refuse to validate your feelings. If they can't say "I'm sorry you're going through this," but insist on saying "It's not that bad, is it?" then you need to walk away from them, because they aren't respecting your feelings. They only serve to make you feel worse and alone in your feelings. If they truly care, they will want to know how they can help you and not invalidate what you're going through.

Another thing you can try is to do something nice for yourself. It doesn't have to cost money, it could simply be taking a walk through a park or watching a movie you've been wanting to see. If you don't feel like you can leave your home, call a friend who understands what you're going through and ask them to bring some soda to go with the popcorn you're making and watch the movie together. Be sure to emphasize soda or something else non-alcoholic, as turning to alcohol will only end up making you feel worse. Also, if your dysphoria is so bad that it is negatively impacting your life – such as causing you to miss work or preventing you from leaving your home – call a trans-friendly therapist or a counselor and go see them. If there isn't one local, get on the internet and find an online support group.

If you aren't able to afford hormones or surgery, then try to find inventive ways to begin a "Transition Fund" for yourself. The internet has many possibilities; from GoFundMe.com where you can raise money, to sites such as Fiverr.com, where you can put your talents to work for others. Are you artistic? Can you write? Are you good at grammar or adept with data entry? Are you bilingual or have musical talent? Do you have any business expertise such as advising, consulting or market research? Any one of these talents can generate an income for yourself online, and you don't have to leave your home to do it. When it came time for me to find the money, I sold my car to pay for surgery. Sometimes we have to give up something in order to obtain what is most important to us.

Even after a medical transition – after hormones, hair removal for women, and even surgeries – not every transgender person is happy with the results. When a person lives any significant amount of time being unhappy and disgusted with their body and having the negative self-image, it's tough trying to see one's self more positively. Again, this isn't unique to being transgender. Many people who have been substantially overweight for many years and lose that weight still see themselves as "fat," and will often end up underweight and ill because all they can see is their former self in the mirror. On any given day you could be on Cloud Nine because you feel "right" in your medically-transitioned body, but then your good spirits are abruptly halted when someone unintentionally misgenders you, and you begin a spiraling journey downwards back into depression.

Perhaps the most important advice I can give you is

– simply try to love yourself as you are, and know that your body is not you – your body is only the exterior. I don't say this to minimize the fact that it's not the body you desire or envision for yourself, but it is what you have at the moment, and agonizing over this fact will only give you more pain and mental anguish. I do know what you're going through. I've been there, and I've done all the wrong things to try to "fix" it. The only thing that got me through was trying to achieve and keep the self-love I so desperately needed for myself until I was able to pursue a medical transition. I had to get to a place of being OKAY with *me*. It wasn't easy, but in the end I was able to live day to day with less mental suffering and more in tune with the positive things and people around me. It took me over thirty adult years to get there, then I had to wait several more years before I could medically transition due to medical issues I was coping with. I can only hope and have faith that you find peace much sooner than I did for myself.

4

Gotta Get These Things Off My Chest

"A sense of humor is the best indicator that you will recover; it is often the best indicator that people will love you. Sustain that and you have hope." ~ Andrew Solomon, *The Noonday Demon: An Atlas of Depression*

GET TO KNOW a transman or a transwoman, and you will inevitably hear stories of their transition. What better way for us as transgender people to educate others than to share our stories with them. It makes us real, it makes us human, and it helps with opening their hearts and minds.

Some aspects of transition are painful, some are easy, and some are funny. There are steps involved, but there's no particular order, nor one right way to transition. The experience is a different one for all who pursue it. Some of the things we all have in common, however, are the milestones. Those specific times where we each consider that particular "moment" when we have reached a goal we had set for ourselves.

For some, it's that first dose of cross-gender hormones…that exciting moment when the medical transition has finally become a reality. For transmen, the top surgery, I believe, is one of the more important milestones (after that first shot of Testosterone).

Sometimes the hormones are the big one for guys, but for others it is the surgery that is the significant one. Speaking for myself, I'm a little guy but I had those darned BIG protrusions sticking out of my chest. When I say big, I mean large DD's, on a guy only 5'3" tall.

Binding is probably THE MOST uncomfortable thing a human being can do to themselves. Not only do we wear the compression shirt or vest after pretzel-ing ourselves into it – arms splayed in contortions we never dreamed of – we then put on an undershirt, followed by a loose fitting over-shirt. Try that sometime in 115 degrees, which is what I was doing in the months prior to my surgery.

Even with facial hair and the physical changes our faces go through, even if we can "pass" in public – which we do fairly quickly, easily, and without many issues – for those of us with C cups and larger, we still have the issue of not being able to effectively hide our "liabilities". Even the smaller guys still have to bind, so I'm not saying it's easy for them, it's just not as difficult. But the same emotional aspect of having breasts and having to bind exists no matter what size we are.

We can't just, for instance, go for a swim with the guys, because, well, you got it – guys don't swim with two to three layers of shirts on. We can't remove our outer shirts when it gets warmer, or wear the tank tops like the other guys. We can't go to the gym and dress in front of other men, we have to either already be in our gym clothes, or leave sweaty, or find a private corner, or a time when the gym's not so busy.

We ask questions, we research, and we find out every single, little tiny detail of what the surgery will be like; coming out of it, recovery, and life afterward. We celebrate with each other, congratulate each other, envy those who have had the surgery, and support those who haven't. We point the pre-operative men to the best affordable binders, and pass our used binders along to those who cannot afford the new ones.

You get the picture. Our top surgery is THE surgery that is probably the most cherished, the most valued, the most emotionally and mentally satisfying aspect of our transition. We count the days to the surgery. We let everyone know, every day, just how many days left until we get these two problems off our chests.

We have our surgery, we wake up from the anesthesia, and immediately look DOWN, and what do you know? It's FLAT! We rejoice in our drug-induced state, we smile, we utter unintelligible words describing our excitement of confirming that we are men and it shows to the rest of the world. We will put on our shirts (of course, we all go out and buy new dress shirts) and we see that they fit correctly for the first time and for the rest of our lives.

Some have asked me, what were my first words out of surgery? I was told I kept asking *"how much?"* over and over, until my wife and the nurses finally figured out that I wanted to know how much those removed "problems" weighed! I guess I needed to know that I'd lost weight or something, I am not sure. What I do know is that I felt even more of a man that day, and no one could ever take that away from me.

Several people have asked me about the pain I had from my top surgery. I know that everyone is different as far as pain-tolerance levels, but I consider myself somewhat of a "wimp" when it comes to pain. I describe my own pain from surgery like this: Think about stubbing your barefoot toe really hard against a chair leg or something. I'm sure you know how excruciating this feels (especially if you break it, but even if you don't, it feels like you did.) Now...*my surgery pain did not feel this bad.*

Yes, it hurt, I can't say that it didn't. It was really uncomfortable the first two or three days. My movements were minimal. As the days went on it got better, except for where the drains were under my arms. They hurt right up until they were removed at Day 10. But I was still able to get up and get around okay, I just had to be very careful about turning, stooping, reaching, etc... and definitely the discomfort of sleeping on my back grew old quickly when I was used to sleeping on my side. After a few days, I did my best to turn partially onto one side or the other propped with pillows. As soon as those drains came out, it wasn't so bad.

The surgeon had put a medical compression vest on me, and I wore it until the day the drains came out. I had no outer stitches; it was simply "glued" on the outside, so there were/are no major scars. I did have extreme swelling on the right side, and the numbness & tingling/burning took months to disappear from that side. I was very careful for the first month after surgery to not lift *anything*. I couldn't reach upwards for at least two to three weeks without feeling it pulling, so I put everything I needed on counters at shoulder level or lower. But none of it was *too much* pain – it hurt, but it wasn't at all as bad as I had expected. I never used anything except regular Extra Strength Tylenol after leaving the surgical center.

Many transmen ask me if there is anything they should be aware of during the recovery period after chest reconstruction surgery. From what I've heard from several transwomen who've had breast augmentation work done, it's good advice for them, also. Along with following all of the post-op instructions that will be given to you, here is what I found to be the most valuable instruction of all.

The most important thing to consider during recovery is to have *every single thing* that you might possibly need down at waist-to-chest level – nothing higher, nothing lower. You will be up doing things within a few days, but your arm motion will be very restricted for a few weeks. Reaching up to get a plate or a can from the upper cupboards is a no-no. Reaching down is also not good. Put everything you need on the counters and kitchen table. Food, plates, coffee, etc.

Rearrange the fridge to put the most accessed items at the top level (assuming you have to bend down to get into it if your freezer is on top.)

You cannot lift anything until your doctor says it's okay. I'm sure you'll think you can, you'll want to. But, no, don't. You can't risk breaking your stitches, or pulling apart freshly healing skin.

Wear easy on/off clothing, and there should be no stretching of your arms to get into T-shirts the first few days or even longer, at least until the drains are removed. Open front, button up shirts are best. Besides, don't you want to leave your shirt open to show off your new bare chest (especially after the bandages and drains are removed?)

I cannot emphasize enough this next piece of advice – ask for help! It may seem like it's a minor thing, and you might try to convince yourself it isn't too heavy, or too far above your head. Do you really want to risk it, though? Check your pride and ego at the door and ask someone for assistance. They will understand and be more than happy to help, knowing in doing so they are helping you heal faster and without complication.

Lastly, laugh along the way. You went through a lot of emotional and physical pain to get to this place – now live it up and ignore the irritating things that will happen after (any) surgery!

5

My Not-So-Mommy-Dearest

"We aren't the weeds in the crack of life. We're the strong, amazing flowers that found a way to grow in the most challenging conditions." ~ Jeanne McElvaney, *Spirit Unbroken: Abby's Story*

I WRITE THIS chapter to share some of my background that really has nothing to do with my being transgender, but has everything to do with who I was and who I am now. I think many people look at a person's past to see what influenced them, especially when it pertains to the transgender journey. But being transgender is only a small part of a person's life and there is so much more to a person than their gender.

My mother was a scary monster to me when I was young. I never knew from day to day, or even from moment to moment, what her disposition was going to be. Would she be depressed, lying in bed in her room for days? Or would she be on the living room floor throwing a temper tantrum, or screaming at me to spend more time on a section of a piano composition I was learning? Or maybe, would it be a rare occasion where she was showing me how to make pineapple upside-down cake and we would laugh loud and long together as flour went everywhere?

Whatever the occasion, it never failed that she would open up the "special" kitchen cupboard, the one where she kept all of her doctor's prescriptions, and then proceed to open a few random bottles to remove some pills she would then take. Though we had ample space in our double-sink bathroom cabinets, she chose to boldly keep her medicines in a kitchen cupboard. They filled the bottom shelf of one cupboard, with the bottles being labeled by various pharmacies and having several different doctor's names on them.

If anyone from outside of the family had ever seen this shelf of pharmaceuticals, they would have known there was something seriously wrong with my mother, and I don't necessarily mean physically. It was the Sixties and Seventies, however, so "prescription drug addicts" were not something that people spoke about or even thought about. Most people were too concerned with Vietnam, the Summer of Love, Charles Manson, Woodstock, and the Civil Rights Movement among other life-changing and culture-defining events.

The first time I recall the subject of drugs being discussed with seriousness was after Diane Linkletter's suicide when her father, Art, began his anti-drug campaign. Art Linkletter, (1912-2010) was a radio and television personality many years ago. I sat in a classroom with my fellow grade school students shortly after her death and watched Mr. Linkletter blame his daughter's death on the effects of LSD, (as well as blaming the Beatles, and Dr. Timothy Leary, who

Linkletter claimed was an unwitting part of her "murder" as Leary was an advocate of psychedelic drugs.) She had none in her system on the night she jumped to her death, but we learned that day about flashbacks and the dangers of drugs.

To hear my mother talk of this ache or that pain, you'd believe the poor woman was suffering from some wicked flesh-eating bacteria or horrible bone disease or some other grave illness. I'm not saying that she didn't have a few legitimate physical issues through the years I lived with her, and, as well, I was hearing it well into my adulthood (though our times of getting together were few and far between.) One of her favorite stories to tell were of the eighteen hemorrhoids removed during a surgery, some "as big as a man's thumb" as she would exclaim. I can't recall to be able to accurately count how many surgeries or hospital stays (most, I believe, completely unnecessary,) that my mother had during those years. I thought she was a hypochondriac, because I had learned that word in grade school, and it was just a fact of life in our home.

I didn't know the meaning of Munchausen's Syndrome when I was growing up, nor did I know what that Syndrome was "by Proxy" (of which I was an unsuspecting, unlucky recipient.) I didn't realize, either, that she was a die-hard opiate drug addict. After all, it was just not discussed anywhere at that time.

Munchausen's Syndrome (I learned many years later although I knew it to be true, I just didn't have the name for it,) is where a person feigns a disease, illness, or psychological trauma to draw attention or sympathy to themselves. And, wow, was she good at it. She was definitely a "frequent flyer" at local hospitals and medical clinics. She had everyone around convinced of her ailments. Except that I wasn't convinced. I couldn't say whether my father or my sister were convinced or not. They dealt with it in their own ways, and there was never a discussion between any of us about it.

"Munchausen's Syndrome by Proxy" means that a person will abuse another person, typically their child, to gain attention or sympathy for themselves. "Oh… look at my poor daughter, she has a brain defect." That was her favorite one for me. After subjecting me to dozens of doctors in three different states, multiple psychiatrists, Naturopaths, and other health professionals for about five years, finally, when I was seventeen a doctor at Stanford decided that my EEG (back when they stuck a whole bunch of little pins in one's head) showed that I had Temporal Lobe Epilepsy. This was a popular but not yet fully understood diagnosis in the 1970s to explain irrational sudden cognitive behaviors. It was later learned that this was a bogus diagnosis given by doctors due to the lack of having any other diagnoses to explain behaviors. I was subjected to three more of those somewhat painful EEG's during that last year of living at home. I'm pretty sure my head was a pincushion.

You need to understand that my mother had me at the doctor's office almost as much as she took herself. As I wrote in an earlier chapter, there were plenty of trips. It was close to once a week that we took trips to one doctor or another, as well as more than one hospital stay for "tests." She was always finding something "wrong" with me. I have already written about when I was little; I was pigeon-toed, so leg braces were procured and there was the matter of me not sitting up straight enough at the table, so the back brace was in order.

When I entered puberty I had terrible acne, so there were the weekly trips to the hour-long appointment with the dermatologist who would use his cold, metal instruments to pop each and every one of my zits, then rub alcohol on the open sores to cleanse them. There was the "Severe Vitamin Deficiency" diagnosis (yeah, right) and the fourteen vitamin pills each morning and evening which had placated her for a short time (maybe a few months) until she realized the "problems" were still happening and not getting better, so she needed to find other outlets to make sure people knew how "good" of a mother she was.

There were the psychiatrists who would spend their forty minutes trying to get me to open up and talk to them, and the ten minutes of them telling my parents everything I had just told them in "confidence," which was then followed by the punishments for the "lies" I had told the doctor. There was the trip to the State

Mental Hospital to see if perhaps I should be committed. I was twelve, and I was excited at the thought of being able to live away from my mother, away from the horrors she was inflicting upon me, and away from the summers being forced to spend time with my grandfather alone and vulnerable with no one to turn to for help.

These are just examples of a childhood full of medical traumas forced on me. To my mother, the "brain defect" was the answer to her prayers. Leaving California behind as we drove back to our hometown in a neighboring State, my mother promptly dumped all of the psychiatric medicines I'd been taking, along with the twenty-six various daily vitamin pills I'd been subjected to for the nearly two years prior to then due to the "Severe Vitamin Deficiency" I supposedly had. These were replaced with yet another drug that was supposed to help cure me. I don't recall which drug it was, I just remember it being some sort of narcotic. Through the years, I probably took most of the popular anti-psychotic and mood-altering drugs known to man during that time period; I do remember several of them by name.

She began calling everyone she knew to tell them about her daughter's "Brain Defect." She never used the word "epilepsy," she just let them assume I was mentally challenged. This, in her eyes, explained all the issues and problems that I had caused her for seventeen years. It didn't, of course, and it only took me a day or two to continue displaying "irrational behaviors" to prove that she and the latest doctors were wrong.

Growing up, it seems like my mother was either laid up in her bed or in a hospital for much of my grade school years. I remember several "housekeepers" as she liked to call them; however, they were nothing more than nannies. They were there to watch my sister and me while our mother spent days and weeks hidden in her bedroom. The majority of the housekeeping was done by my sister and me as our daily and weekly chores.

She was mostly in bed in my high school years, except for the multiple trips per month to doctors. I recognize this now as severe depression, which wasn't being treated except by her own hand with the many varieties of opiate prescriptions for "pain" that she'd managed to obtain from the various doctors. This was before everything was computerized, before these things could be tracked and controlled.

When I was in a group art therapy session in my late thirties, our therapist handed each of us a large sheet of white drawing paper, and several crayons of various colors were spread in the center of the table we surrounded. She told us to draw an early memory. My brain was flooded with memories, and it took me a while to realize how to draw those negative images. When I did, the crayons started flying across the drawing paper as I spewed out all the anger I felt towards my mother.

My drawings centered around my mother's bed, her lying in it with several different items surrounding her and the bed. Mind you, not all of the items were actually in or around the bed with her, but each of them were a memory associated with her. I drew a hairbrush, for the hard pink plastic one she had given me for Christmas, then beat me with it until it broke in two.

I also drew a Bible. Did I mention she was an ultra-religious freak? She would post a Bible verse on the refrigerator each day, and we were required to memorize it. As well, there was the requirement to read a clipped newspaper article of some disaster, or death, or some other negative something of the "Devil's doing" each day. Her Bible was in bed with her, or near her much of the time. She rarely went to church, since she was so busy being sick with some new illness, but she made sure her children attended church. Always twice on Sundays for a total of five hours, and at least one evening a week, usually Wednesdays, for another two hours, not to mention every special event or occasion or Bible study that was going on at any given time.

But, now, I've been sidetracked. Back to my drawing for the therapist. I drew a kitchen cooking pot, filled with water. She had discovered by accident one day that throwing a pot of (what started out that time as cold) water on me when I was yelling at her would stop me instantly. Yes, it did get warmer and warmer until it was not quite hot enough to leave scars.

I drew quite a few prescription bottles with pills scattered over and around the bed, and a box of tissues because inevitably she'd be crying over something, and of course the telephone was in her hand. It was the old rotary-dial black phone in those years. In later years, she upgraded to the cordless ones so she could actually walk around and talk. If you stood outside her bedroom door, you could hear her talk and cry for hours about all the health problems she had, or what her poor daughter had most recently gotten herself into and what the doctors thought it might be. To this day, I wonder who in their right mind would stay on the phone and listen to her over and over again. Actually, I met one of those women when I was older and found that she was basically a "clone" of my mother, so it made sense how the two of them got along so well together.

Lastly, I drew my version of "The Silent Treatment". I depicted this with a pair of earmuffs over her ears and a cloth around her mouth. If she was mad at me or my dad she would sometimes go days, even a couple of weeks or more, of simply not talking to whomever her anger was directed towards. I can't count the number of times I would have to relay messages between her and my dad, and I'm sure he had to do the same for me. She just refused to talk to the person she was angry with. It was that simple.

Some people have asked me if I endured other physical abuses when growing up, so I'll share just a bit of that here. Corporal punishment was legal at home and in schools in the generation and the location I grew up in. My dad's belts were the common method of discipline from him, as well as a switch from a Willow tree in our backyard (I had to go pick the switch, which he would then cut off the tree and use on me.) Fortunately, his spankings were on my bottom where they belonged. He also ceased spanking me when I was around twelve or thirteen.

My mother had different devices for inflicting punishments; from hairbrushes to rulers and any other hard objects she could grab quickly and easily. By the time I was entering puberty, she obtained a paddle board that was just under three inches wide, and maybe fifteen inches long. It depicted a cartoon picture of a deer and a bear with the painted words *"For the cute little deer with the bear behind"* and the handle boasted the words "Grip here firmly in case of frustration." Over the years, the words and pictures on the paddle wore off from repeated use. Well into my young teenage years, this paddle was my mother's choice of punishment on my bare behind (and anywhere else she could reach as I struggled to get away.)

One day I'd had enough (I was perhaps fifteen or sixteen,) and I grabbed the paddle from her and threw it down. I pinned her against the wall of my bedroom and wrapped my hands around her neck in my anger. I squeezed hard, and as she began choking, my father walked into the room, folded his arms across his chest and said to me very calmly, "If you kill her, I'll kill you." I guess my sense of self-preservation took over, and I loosened the grip on my mother's neck. As often as I had suicidal thoughts as a youth, I guess I found the thought of my life ending by someone else's doing was something I wanted to avoid.

My mother went on to other forms of physical punishment after that, including the pots of hot water I mentioned earlier. Many times I went to school with bruises, and once even a broken rib (confirmed once broken when I became an adult) from my punishments, but when the school advisors asked about them and I would tell the truth – that the injuries were from my parents – nothing was ever done to protect me. I won't write more about this, but now I've answered those who have asked, and it gives you a bit more insight into my experiences.

I learned to hate this woman. The hate began growing when I was old enough to realize something wasn't right with her, and I was generally the person she took her anger out on. I responded in kind – anger for anger. Temper for temper. Scream for scream. I went further and I broke things, I punched walls, and I took it out on myself pounding on my own head and eventually other self-harming behaviors to release the pain I was living with. I will touch more on the aspect of self-harm in a later chapter.

The writer, James Baldwin, once wrote:

"I imagine one of the reasons people cling to their hates so stubbornly is because they sense, once hate is gone... they will be forced to deal with pain" (Baldwin, 1984).

How true this is. I hung on to my hatred for my mother for many years, which ultimately influenced nearly every action and direction I took in my life until I was almost forty years old. My hatred and consequential anger were the driving forces which propelled me through those years, keeping me from feeling the pain hidden deep down inside my soul. Some of that pain, you'll understand, was that of not being born in the body I deeply desired. I did find a way to crawl out of that seemingly bottomless pit, and I'll share it with you as you continue to read upcoming chapters.

6

Adoption "Stories"

"Do not believe in anything simply because you have heard it. Do not believe in anything simply because it is spoken and rumored by many. Do not believe in anything simply because it is found written in your religious books. But after observation and analysis, when you find that anything agrees with reason and is conducive to the good and benefit of one and all, then accept it and live up to it." ~ *The Buddha*

ADOPTION ISN'T a rare or unusual thing; it has taken place for many years and helped to fulfill the dreams of many young parents who were unable to bear children of their own, or perhaps simply to give a child a chance at life in a good home. Many adoptees know the story of their adoption, and many express and feel gratitude towards their adoptive parents for giving them a good childhood.

I'm not one of those. I can't say there was nothing good in my childhood, because there were some good things, as I mentioned earlier. However, the "bad stuff" far outweighed the "good stuff", and it wasn't until I was in my late thirties, nearly forty, during therapy that I recognized most of the good.

My own adoption story has a twist. You see, it's not just *one* story. It is one (or none) of multiple stories all told to me by a mentally ill, drug-addicted mother in her misguided and harmful attempts to try to control me as well as other circumstances beyond her control.

I'm telling my story, or rather, "stories" in order to help you, the reader, understand even more of the type of home life I had as a youth. There were so many facets and types to the abuses I endured, each adding a layer of hate and anger inside me as I tried to simply be the person I was. That person, that *child*, was not the girl that everyone saw on the outside. But in the Sixties for a child not yet in their teenage years, there were no words nor concepts of gender except in strictly enforced binary roles that we were all expected to live by.

My adoption papers stated I was female, as did my birth certificate. As far as anyone knew because a doctor, or perhaps a midwife, (I was never told) had seen my genitals and made this grievously erroneous declaration, "It's a Girl!" I was for all intents and purposes a girl, and that's what they expected me to act like and grow up to be.

I've always known that I was adopted. My mother and father had both told me from the earliest time I can remember. They always let me know how "special" I was, and that they had chosen me since they had both especially wanted a daughter. I also knew by the time I was in grade school that my adoptive mother could not have children due to a hysterectomy just prior to me coming along, and that I came from a state adoption facility when I was two months old.

When I was young, I was told by my adoptive mother that my birth mother and father were a young married couple who were very poor and they had made the choice to give me a better life with someone who could provide for all my needs. I was told, too, that I was an answer to prayer, that I was the daughter my (adoptive) mom and dad had always wanted. Little did they know that my genitals were not an accurate representation of who I really was.

As I grew older and entered my early teen years, the story of my birth and background changed a few times. To make excuses for my erratic behaviors, which were now occurring daily at home, in school and in church, my adoptive mother let me know, as well as she let everyone know, that my birth mother had been a drug addict, and had experienced some serious mental problems.

This, of course, explained her daughter's problems (for a time, anyway) and took the blame off of her. "My poor daughter, her birth mother had so many problems, and these problems are hereditary. See? They were handed down to her from her birth mother. See what I must endure? See how strong I am to deal with what God has placed in my care? I know He'll never give me more than I can handle. But it's so hard, let me tell you."

A few years later, the story changed once again. I was nineteen years old, had left home a year earlier, and had just begun to search for my birth mother (which wasn't easy – we didn't have Internet back then!) My adoptive mom asked me if I was looking, to which I answered yes (a mistake to tell the truth, I learned.) Lo and behold, she suddenly had something "sad" to tell me.

This time the story I was told was that my mother and father were not married, that he had left her when he found out she was pregnant, leaving her an unwed mother with no means of taking care of a child. I was told she'd been in and out of hospitals and psyche wards and finally, when she was thirty-five (I would have been seventeen,) she had died of cervical cancer. Talk about a mind-screw, right?

Now how about the last time the story changed? I was twenty-two and discontent and angry with the way the stories had changed and evolved during my childhood. I approached my adoptive parents one last time telling them (demanding) I wanted the truth. This time I made sure I had both my mom and dad together, as it had always been just my mom telling me the stories while I was growing up.

(On a side note, I don't know if my dad was ever aware of my mom's lies. He was away from home working a lot when I was young, even into my teens. I'm guessing it's because he wasn't able to handle being around my mom, but I'll never know for sure. I wasn't emotionally or mentally capable of talking to him honestly and openly prior to him passing away suddenly when I was thirty-five years old.)

My mother was silent this last time I asked while my dad told me that my birth mom and dad were indeed married when I was born and that I had two siblings; a brother and a sister. I was told that my mom was good looking (so they met her?) and that they were both intelligent and well educated. Yet, when I asked why my birth parents gave me up for adoption they gave no explanation. They claimed they were not told any reason by the adoption agency.

Through all those years my mom would tell me over and over how "special" I was, and ask why did I take that for granted? Why did I not understand that God had answered her prayers for a beautiful young daughter to raise? And through all those years my only answer to her was a silent one known only to myself, and one filled with contempt and sarcasm for her and for the life I had with her… "Yeah, right."

I never did find out the truth, or perhaps one of the stories really was the truth. My birth state finally opened up adoption records so adoptees could find information on their birth parents. I did send away for mine years later and was able to find my birth mother's name. By this time, however, I'd come to terms with the "loss" of my childhood truth, and had mentally acquiesced to the conflicting stories which had played over and over in my mind for far too many years.

My original birth certificate, of course, confirmed the worst when I read the box where my name should be…   "Baby   Girl".

7

(Trans) Gender Primer

"It is the movement across a socially imposed boundary away from an unchosen starting place— rather than any particular destination or mode of transition— that best characterizes the concept of 'transgender'" ~ Susan Stryker, *Transgender History*

BABY GIRL. Oh, how that resonated through me and brought the reality of socially constructed gender to the forefront of my thoughts. It wasn't until I really started paying attention, listening to others and researching the aspects of transitioning and the transgender community that I learned the difference between sex and gender and about assigned sex and affirmed gender. Many have heard the following from various sources, but there are those who may be reading this book who have not had the opportunity to learn and understand what the trans community already knows. Therefore, I will cover it here and will continue to educate society as long as I see there is a need for the information.

Sex is a designation based on biology; gender is socially constructed and expressed. It's defined by society and expressed by individuals as they interact with others, and can change as one learns to act masculine or feminine. Author Julia T. Wood says "What gender means and how we express it depend on a society's values, beliefs and preferred ways of collective life" (Wood, 2012). Gender can vary across cultures and within a culture.

In mainstream societies on a global scale the two are still being confused and conflated, creating the illusion that there are two and only two sexes, and these sexes determine gender as being male and female. In these mistaken perceptions of gender, society stereotypes men and women seeing them as two distinct, opposite groups.

Transgender people know the difference. We know that how we view ourselves – our perception of ourselves – is our gender identity. We know that who we are attracted to sexually is completely irrelevant in the self-defining and declaration of our gender. We also know this can, and does, cause great confusion to our peers, families and coworkers when we come out to them as being a transgender individual.

It's interesting when you look at gender on a deeper level; specifically, the differences in behavior and attitudes rather than the biological or physical differences. I believe when we are born, there is no innate significant difference between any two children. From the moment of conception and when the child comes out of the womb and is announced and assigned as a boy or a girl, however, that child has already been defined as being on one or the other end of that binary scale.

More often than not (although it's slowly changing as parents are becoming more aware,) that child will be subjected to certain social cues that begin defining their gender. The child will be given certain colors of clothing, certain types of toys and be treated differently depending on his or her sex while growing up. Behavior and attitudes will be displayed and defined by parents, siblings, peers, teachers and eventually employers.

What I'm saying is that a person's gender, because of their assigned sex and although it is an ingrained self-identity, is being defined from birth onwards, both socially and culturally. These social cues that surround them – these subtle, as well as blatant, expectations of males and females – are what transgender people have to struggle with as they mature.

Children immediately begin to learn gender by watching and listening to the interactions of people around them as well as how those people interact with them. The child learns to model these behaviors. As they get older, these gendered social cues have already been established within the child's brain, whether or not it is conflicting yet with their inner since of identity. Boys learn to communicate with competition, learn control, to solve problems and get attention. Girl's play involves a lot of talking, and relationships are cooperative. The child has learned the patriarchal view of life and their forms of communication stem from their social environment.

In the same token, there are those who do not conform to the typical male/female behaviors expected from them – for instance, trans people, usually from a younger age, exhibit behaviors of the "opposite" sex, although they are just being themselves and modeling after what feels comfortable to them. Either way, however, we learn from our environment. Leaving us, sadly, with the truth that there are typically male-specific and female-specific behaviors which conform to the socially accepted norm.

Androgynous people as they mature begin ignoring the social and cultural expectations and the stereotypes of gender. This enables them to view not only themselves, but the world itself from an entirely new and unique perspective. They not only challenge gendered social behaviors and expectations, but they actually negate them, too. In doing so, they have freed their inner self identity to simply be "comfortable" in their own skin. These people may not feel either male or female, and may identify as non-binary, genderqueer or gender-fluid, and many consistently and doggedly confront and dispute the expected social norms in order to be themselves. I don't believe society is quite as "afraid" of this group of people as they are of those who step "over" into the "opposite" role they were born into.

Speaking generally, and not for all – transgender people don't seem to experience the same social success. In fact, one can look at the statistics of suicide rates, murders, losses of jobs, homes, family and peers of transgender individuals to see this is true. I believe that society is much more accepting of androgynous individuals and, therefore, those individuals have the freedoms of expression, passion and behaviors not afforded to transgender people. I tend to think this is because transgender people are still typed and trapped by other's views of their sex rather than their gender both before and after transition and expectations of binary, biological gender attributes cause fear and uncertainty in mainstream population.

Appearances make a definite impression on people, whether it's a physical body appearance, or the way someone is dressed, or their mannerisms that may stand out (waving their arms/hands when speaking makes them get noticed more, for instance.) It's been proven that people can tell a lot about a person from a fraction of a second when viewing a photo of the person, including being able to tell whether they are gay or not.

Prejudices can immediately be formed, even subconsciously, when meeting someone due to their appearance; which then can distort one's perception about anything that person may have to say, taking that stereotype as a nonverbal behavior itself and making a judgment.

Freud (1856-1939) believed we are all shaped and defined by our genitals, even going so far as labeling stages of development in life in psychosexual terms, (all focused around the penis, of course.) Karen Horney (1885-1952), a German psychologist, disagreed with Freud's theory of "penis envy", and introduced the term "womb envy." She believed that the reason men feel superior to women is because of their jealousy of women's ability to reproduce.

I believe that socially and culturally, our anatomy defines perceptions and imposes expectations. I believe the "self" is at the core of one's being, and I believe that the internalized dialogue individuals have with "self" due to other's perceptions and interactions with us and how we innately *feel* is what serves to define us, not our anatomy. When we don't conform to standards, we realize that we are gender variant and, in many cases, we are transgender and/or transsexual. We defy other's ideas of our own destiny.

"Destiny" is a strong word; it means a power that is believed to control what happens in the future. Destiny is only as powerful as the individual(s) assume it to be an entity. Unfortunately, our society is one that perpetuates binary gender attributes to not only living organisms, but even to non-living items (ships, countries and cars are a "she", yet while when seeing an insect in the house, gender unknown, the automatic thought is "put him outside". Or in my case, run away from it!)

Human language and behaviors shape gender perceptions, values and beliefs from the moment our brains become aware of our environment. Henri Tajfel (1919-1982) defined social identity theory, which is a person's self-concept derived from one's membership in a social group. This theory, I believe, is the most accurate in the "destiny" of how one defines, and is defined.

The most relevant example I can give is a transgender person who consciously and unconsciously counteracts and challenges the social perception of binary gender. It is only because of people's perceptions and beliefs which are formed by their culture that discrimination even exists.

Many people have approached the question of "what is the difference between transgender and transsexual?" It's a discussion that circulates now and again around the trans community, so it's not just a casual question or inquisitive one from those who are not transgender. It is, sadly, the apparently never-ending debate of the differences between the meanings of "transsexual" and "transgender", and who "is" and who "isn't" either or both.

Not only do these discussions seem to harm and divide our own community, they make it a more difficult obstacle to overcome for those who are not transgender, and who want to learn about our community. The discussions inspire anger and animosity and, more often than not, they create enemies in a community that needs all the allies it can muster, with allies meaning ourselves included.

For those who want to learn about the transgender community, here's the basic, simple truth, or at least, my perspective on it. For those who are trans, whether or not you agree is up to you, and if you think something differently, you can write your own book about it, because my perception isn't up for debate.

The following sentence is for the people who are sincerely trying to learn about us.

We are trans (*insert-either-ending-here-that-makes-you-more-comfortable*) people.

Whether or not we have had surgeries or have taken hormones. Whether we live publicly or stealth. Whether we are active in the transgender community or we have withdrawn from activism and live quiet lives. We were each born in a body we felt was not right for us. We all have our obstacles to overcome, and we all have the inherent need to feel accepted as our true, authentic self.

Some transpeople call themselves transgender, while others claim the word transsexual, yet others include both when describing themselves. The word "transsexual" is a medical term which indicates that one is pursuing or has pursued a medical transition. Transgender has become an "umbrella" term, which captures any gender-variant person on the full gender spectrum including those who medically transition, those who don't, those who feel they are both male and female, and those who feel like they are no gender or androgynous.

I am very open with who I am. I am *me*, Michael Eric Brown. If you need a label to define me, I am a transman. I happen to be a transsexual man and I am also comfortable being included in the spectrum of the transgender umbrella.

I make it a point to educate the public, even those within the LGBT community, not only reminding them that we exist but that we are also human beings who deserve the same respect and equality that any other human being deserves, whatever label we use.

Everyone is entitled to their own individual interpretations, but the way I see it – we are all trans people, and who gives a flying fig whether the ending is "gender" or "sexual" when both of those are labels people coined for those of us who are trans individuals whether medically transitioning or not.

Trans is trans - regardless of the ending, whether transgender or transsexual, and we were all born in a body that didn't conform to our idea or inner identification of who we are. Society tried defining us, and we could not, or would not, conform. To those in the trans community, if you need a label to define yourself, take it, use it and own it. If you don't want to label yourself, that's certainly acceptable, too. If you give someone else a label, you are putting them into a "box" that you have defined, and it is simply unacceptable.

8

Innocence Lost

"Religion has the capacity to silence critical thinking and create blindness in entire groups of people. It can infect the minds of followers so completely as to allow the most egregious sexual acts against children and others to go unchallenged for centuries." ~ Darrell Ray, *Sex & God: How Religion Distorts Sexuality*

MY MOTHER SAID to me one day, "Go down and get your grandfather, tell him it's time for breakfast." I was close to four years old, my new baby sister had been adopted just a few months before, and my mother was tending to her while she was also finishing preparing our breakfast.

It was a beautiful summer morning, and I was wearing my favorite outfit; a pair of pants, a T-shirt and tennis shoes. I ran through the house, down the stairs, out through the sliding glass door, and across the yard. We had two acres, and my grandfather was staying in a small travel trailer about a half an acre away.

He had been there only a few days, having come to visit from a small southern town on the other side of the continent. Each summer, we either spent a few weeks over there with him and my grandmother, or one or both would come to stay with us for a while.

After this trip, it was more likely you'd find us on the east side of the continent staying with them, since traveling got easier when my younger sister was no longer an infant.

As I neared the trailer and I went around the front of it towards the side, I saw that the door was open. I stopped suddenly, and hesitated. I was not looking forward to seeing my grandfather face to face. Not only was he a big man, well over 6 feet tall and likely 240 pounds or more, his demeanor and attitude were just as imposing with an attitude of haughty authority. This was the kind of man that when he said *"Jump"*, people jumped.

Being a man from the South in a state that is considered part of the "Bible Belt" he, of course, was very involved in his church. Seeing him up at the podium on a Sunday morning was not an unusual sight, boldly pronouncing Scripture or a prayer worthy of the angels clapping their wings, or at least that's how he may have appeared to those in the pews (he did to me.) Mostly to himself and his own ego, I'm sure, but as a small child, I thought he was a special man anointed by the Lord, and I believed everything he said.

Which was a sad mistake to trust him so explicitly. Away from the church, when it was just he and I alone, I still believed him even when I was as old as twelve when he would exclaim in short, warm, smelly breaths "I thank Thee, O Lord, for the gift of this sweet, beautiful soft child. Thank you for the perfect body you have blessed her with, the firm, sweet budding breasts..." OK, gag me. You've got a picture in your mind now, and you may as well try to forget it, because no, it's not pretty.

So you can understand my hesitation when I was moments away from seeing my grandfather that summer morning. "But wait," you ask, "didn't you say you were not even four years old?" Yes, and I already had experienced his "fascination" with me. Little did I know back then that it would continue to go on for many summers, for many years to come.

Back to this summer morning...I proceeded cautiously, quietly, hoping he wouldn't hear me as I came near his open door. He had not heard me, for his back was to me. He was standing at the little kitchen counter with not a stitch of clothing on and was busy with something in front of him that I could not see.

I stood there, quietly frozen, and stared at that giant buck-naked man for a second or two, holding my breath and praying fast and furious in my mind, (after all, God hears all of our thoughts, at least, that's what they told me.) "God, please don't let him see me, *please* don't let him see me!"

I then backed away, cautiously and quietly, back around the way I had come. I was breathing hard and I was sure he'd hear my breaths because I was certain they were coming out in gasps. After a few moments my breathing steadied, and I listened. I heard him inside, but he didn't come out the door and around to the front, so I knew I was safe for the moment.

I wanted to avoid seeing him again, *especially if he were naked,* and for sure I didn't want him turning around to show me his front half. I'd seen it another time, many times, in other places and was not wanting to see it again. I called out to him as loudly as my trembling voice could muster, "Granddaddy? Mommy said breakfast is almost ready." I heard his footsteps move closer to the door which was just around the corner from me. I ran back to the house as fast as I could, knowing for that day, that time, I was safe.

You can only imagine the mess I had to dig through emotionally when I began my healing process. My mother with her issues, my grandfather with his predilection for young girls (I found out many years later that I was just one of many.) I can only say now that in discovering the pain in my past and moving through it and past it, I am blessed to be the person I am today because of and despite it all.

9

Gendered Violence

"It's my view that gender is culturally formed, but it's also a domain of agency or freedom and that it is most important to resist the violence that is imposed by ideal gender norms, especially against those who are gender different, who are nonconforming in their gender presentation." ~ Judith Butler, *Your Behavior Creates Your Gender*

IT'S NOT UNUSUAL for transgender individuals to have experienced sexual abuse as youth, including the abuse being inflicted upon them by family members and acquaintances. Studies have shown that LGBT youth are more likely to be abused sexually than their non-LGBT counterparts (Ray, 2006). One survey suggests that sixty-seven percent of reported sexual assault victims are under eighteen years old, with fourteen percent of those being under age six (Briere & Elliot, 2003). As those who are gender-conflicted grow older, they continue to face higher than average risks of sexual and gendered violence.

I once wrote in an editorial piece, "Gender-based violence is a matter of utmost concern. It occurs locally as well as globally in homes, in the community and in nearly every culture" (Brown, 2015). Although the focus of that particular article was campus sexual assaults, the truth is that gender-based violence is a concern for everyone to stand up against. Violence isn't just limited to violence against women. It occurs whenever there is any type of gender non-conformity, such as with gay men, lesbians, and transgender individuals, even if the orientation or identity is perceived by the perpetrators and not necessarily a fact.

There's been a lot of research over the years and it has shown how the media contributes to real life male violence against women. This can be seen in sexually explicit and suggestive films, video games, music videos and even pro-wrestling. In seeing it all the time, it becomes a "normal" way of thinking, and can easily provoke violence that would not have been there to begin with.

Violence takes many forms, from micro-aggressions and verbal sexual harassment, as well as other forms, including physical bullying, domestic violence, sexual assault and female genital mutilation.

Did you know that one in thirty-three men will be raped in their lifetime (Newsom, 2011), or that fifteen percent of all rapes are of girls under twelve years old (Wood, 2013)? If you're transgender, you've probably seen the statistics published in 2009 that say "Those who expressed a transgender identity or gender non-conformity while in grades K-12 reported alarming rates of harassment (78%), physical assault (35%) and sexual violence (12%); harassment was so severe that it led almost one-sixth (15%) to leave a school in K-12 settings or in higher education" (NGLTF & NCTE, 2009).

Institutional violence, too, occurs in many of our social systems, from within the family to academia, and from hospitals and long-term care facilities to the military. Rape and sexual assault runs rampant in the military, as well as all other institutions.

One personal example of gendered violence in an institutional setting I would like to share is a personal experience which happened to me in a military hospital in 1980. I was nineteen years old in Basic Training, and had discovered a health issue that landed me in the hospital. I was still living as a female at the time, not yet having transitioned to male until many years later.

I knew the medical issue meant I would be discharged from the military, as staying in meant a possibility of being permanently disabled due to the Army's physical demands on their soldiers. I wanted to go home rather than be disabled.

The doctor assigned to me, however, had his own agenda and let it be known one night when he came to my hospital room that the only way he would sign my medical chart to be discharged was to be intimate with him. He did not care that if I were to stay in the Army I would be risking my health for the long term. He climbed on top of me on my bed, but as angry as I was, I felt at the time there was nothing I could do to stop him lest I be sent back to my unit the following day, rather than being homeward bound. The next morning he signed the paperwork, and my paperwork was processed as an honorable medical discharge from the Army.

Violence against transgender people is nothing more than evil. One research study in 2012 stated that almost ninety-eight percent of the trans respondents reported that the physical violence they experienced was due to their gender identity or expression (Testa et al., 2012).

It's also common for the perpetrator to go overboard in an attack on a transperson, because the person is trans and how it makes the perpetrator *feel*. An article in the Journal of Hate Studies states it like this,

> The goal of these attacks is not principally to harm or even to simply murder the victim. Instead, the actions of many perpetrators in antitransgender [sic] hate crimes point to a desire to eradicate the transgender-identified individual *in order to alleviate the perpetrator's disgust and to avenge the sense of betrayal that precipitated the attack* in the first place (Kidd & Witten, 2007, italics mine).

The violence – that's bad enough – but also consider that transgender people will likely be victimized a second and third time after the initial attack by uneducated (or uncaring) law enforcement and hospital personnel.

A 50-year old male-to-female individual shared in a survey "Every time I leave the house I leave with three strikes against me. I can be raped for being a woman. I can be raped and murdered because I am perceived as 'gay' (a drag queen) or I can be violently murdered because I am read as trans" (TLARS, n.d.)

Thinking about all this brings me to my thoughts about therapy, and the importance of it in dealing with all of life's issues, including the aspects of gender violence. I am a strong advocate for therapy not only prior to transition, but during and after, as well as for anyone who has gone through any type of dysfunctional situation, trauma or abuse in their lives.

10

Gatekeepers or Life Givers?

"Before you can live a part of you has to die. You have to let go of what could have been, how you should have acted and what you wish you would have said differently. You have to accept that you can't change the past experiences, opinions of others at that moment in time or outcomes from their choices or yours. When you finally recognize that truth then you will understand the true meaning of forgiveness of yourself and others. From this point you will finally be free." ~ *Shannon L. Alder*

THE NEEDLE on the speedometer was nearing 95 miles per hour as I sped down the California freeway chasing after a woman, my friend, in her car. We had parted just minutes before this, and I was angry with her for telling me she couldn't handle my anger anymore, that she needed some time away from me.

My car was a small compact three years old at the time, and was not made for the speeds I was attempting in my pursuit of her. The front end was lifting and control was difficult, but I was so angry I didn't care about either of these things. Nor did I care about the cars I was weaving around and passing at those excessive speeds, not to mention likely frightening each of those drivers. It was one o'clock in the morning, and I had no business being up and driving around at that time, but there I was doing it.

I had followed her that evening to see where it was she went when she would leave her house late at night, or after she left when we would part. She drove up to Los Angeles from the small beach town where we were living in southern Orange County. She eventually pulled into a popular North Hollywood LGBT bar, got out of her car, and went inside. I parked and followed her in. She was surprised to see me, and even more surprised when I began yelling at her in front of everyone there asking her what the hell she thought she was doing?

Rather than arguing with me or even saying a word, she went back out to her car and drove away towards the freeway. I was right behind her honking my horn incessantly, pulling right up to within inches of her rear bumper even when we entered and sped down the freeway. Once we were near home, she pulled off the freeway onto the exit. She stopped briefly at the stop light, and turned to the right towards her home. As she stopped, with me too close behind her, my foot hit the brake. As my brakes were catching hard, and my horn blaring loudly, I skidded up to the rear of her car, missing the bumper by mere inches. Just as she continued with the turn, I saw two police cruisers in the convenience store parking lot across the intersection. Both officers standing near the cruisers yelled and whistled demandingly in my direction, waving their arms and motioning for me to come across the street to where they were.

As I pulled into a parking space near them and waited for them to reach my car, my anger at once turned to shame. What was I to say? What was my excuse for driving so recklessly and loudly in the middle of the night? I had no answer. When they asked, my only answer was that I was mad and I was trying to get my friend to pull over.

I received a firm warning and what seemed like a very long lecture from them that night. I was then told to go home and cool off. They told me if they ever saw me driving erratically again, I would be arrested and thrown in jail for reckless endangerment and attempted murder. I couldn't tell them I had no home and I was sleeping in my car, so I agreed with them and drove off to somewhere I could park safely for the night and sleep.

I look back on that time and many other similar times through my life up until that point. I remember years of blind rage, anger I could not control. I remember the many times I should have been dead or arrested and in prison because of angry stunts like I pulled that night.

I had just lost my therapist a few weeks earlier, and I had already lost the few friends I had due to my anger. I lost the friend I was chasing that night, and although I tried in the future to make amends, she was unable to forgive me. We haven't spoken or seen each other since that time. All I had left that night was my car and what I could fit inside it to call home.

You're probably wondering by now what I was so angry about, that anger that affected everything I did through my life. To this day, I still can't give you a definite answer. For years, I blamed it on my mother, whose prescription drug habit and mental health issues created hell for me growing up. I blamed it on my grandfather who took my childhood innocence away by the time I was three years old and continued for years.

I blamed my anger on the Church and the people who said I had to live according to their beliefs, or I would be shunned (which I was) and I would go to hell for my sins. I blamed society for telling me that because I was female-bodied that I should be wearing dresses and having babies and shaving my legs. I blamed the drugs that were forced on me to make me behave and the psych doctors for diagnosing me with whatever mental illness was popular that year. Then I blamed the street drugs because I had become a drug addict just like my mother.

I blamed the lesbians around me, because they said I wasn't a part of their community because I still liked men and refused to spell women with a "y" ('womyn', popularly used by feminist lesbians of the time.) I blamed my significant others, each of them, because they weren't able to understand my needs. Though I didn't know it at the time, I was "needy". I couldn't find happiness within myself so I tried to suck it out of them, so much so that I was told by each that I was "suffocating" them. Before they could let me go and be the one to break us up, I walked out of the relationship and on to the next.

When I no longer had any of those things or those people around me, I blamed everyone and every circumstance around me at the time, regardless if anything had been done personally to me or not, because anger was my only coping mechanism. The more anger I displayed, the more punishment and consequences I received, and the more anger I displayed. You get the picture. It was a "Catch-22", and there seemed no way out of that vicious cycle.

Today, years later, I feel sadness that I spent so much of my life in such an abyss of anger. I realize I can't change it, and I have since made amends to all those I was able to reach. I try to explain that the anger came from a place deep within, and that I now feel much of it, along with the dysfunctional circumstances I grew up with, had to do with my feelings of just not fitting in.

I couldn't describe the feelings for all those years because I was spending too much mental energy being angry. I only knew on some subconscious, and perhaps even half-conscious level that I was not who I appeared to be, though that didn't make any sense at all.

Since my transition, I've seen so many transmen come into my life full of this same type of anger. Their tempers are short, they are quick to judge, and they fly off in outbursts at something or someone with the same misguided anger I carried for years. They rebel against any form of authority, their appearance is tough-looking with their excessive tattoos and their many piercings, and when they walk into a room, they capture the attention of everyone in the room usually sending out less-than-positive vibes. They seem to seek out, and crave, this attention from others, no matter if it's negative or positive, as long as it's attention. Whether they are aware they are doing this or not, I'm not sure. I think much of it is on some subconscious level. (By the way, I'm not saying anything negative about tattoos and piercings. I have several tattoos and happen to like them on others. My statement above was regarding the tough-looking exterior due to anger issues. Got it?)

I have witnessed many transmen as well as transwomen in the beginnings of their journeys; I've heard their stories and learned their histories. While trying to avoid generalities, I've seen more transwomen coming from what seems to be a place of shame in their lives, while the men come from a place of anger. It's not something I can write about – the experience of these women – since I don't have the same experience. I can ponder and even ask them about it, but I will never be able to relate to their experience because I came from a place of my own, which is a place that is shared by many transmen.

I only understand from what I've seen and from those I've talked with that we all have come from places that were uncomfortable, even miserable. We've all experienced levels of distress because it came from the same place – within ourselves, consciously or not – it was the knowledge that we did not belong in our own skin.

Each of us has come from another place, another life, and we stepped out into our transition journeys at the time and place that was right for us. Many of us follow the standard procedures to medically transition, which generally starts with finding a therapist. There are the ones who skip this vital part of the process and go directly to the hormones and surgeries.

I call therapy a *vital* part of the process because, as I've stated previously, I am a strong advocate of therapy. I'm not talking about just seeing a therapist for the sole purpose of following the suggested guidelines on the path to obtaining legal hormones, or the coveted "Letters" which we all need to change our legal documentation.

We need to take a look at the places we've each come from – those places of discomfort and stress. So many transgender people jump into the transition process thinking ahead of time that living as their affirmed gender will be the answer to their problems, and they can be themselves, and everything will be happiness and roses from that point forward. They somehow equate "transition" as the "cure". What they don't realize, however, is that those places they came from are still with them, carrying all the emotions and triggers of those experiences.

When they have come from a place where anger and rebellion has been their main coping mechanism, a place which is common to so many transmen, the anger doesn't, and can't, just disappear. It may seem to subside for a time, especially in the beginning as these men begin with their Testosterone shots, and their lives seem to be moving forward as their hairs begin to grow and their voices deepen, and they smile more often.

It isn't long, however, before a circumstance or a situation comes up which is uncomfortable for them, and they react in the same way they've always reacted, in anger. Now they have the Testosterone streaming through their bodies, and because they've heard that Testosterone causes aggressiveness, they blame their excessive anger on the Testosterone. They call it "Testosterone Rage".

(Back to the Blaming Game, right? If you can't blame it on someone or on your past or some other circumstance, blame it on the hormones.)

Hormones are not a "cure" for all the situations and issues we've experienced in our lives. Taking Testosterone or Estrogen will not change what happened to us, nor will it "fix" everything from now on. The hormones will help to align our bodies into more of where our minds are. They will help create the physical changes we have coveted and wished we could have for years. Hormones will also affect us emotionally, and this is where I feel therapy is so vital for transgender people.

For years, many transgender people called therapists the "*gatekeepers*", the ones who we depended on to say "yes" or "no" to access of those hormones we so adamantly desired and needed. The standards have changed now, and therapy isn't a "requirement" anymore, but the issues – the anger and the shame – are still very much alive and present in so many who are seeking hormones.

My suggestion to all those who come to me asking me how to get started on hormones – where can they go, who can they see, how fast can it happen – is always the same. I answer them with a request that they share with me about their life, and what brought them to thinking it was time for them to start hormones.

They do, and they talk about their past, and the people in it, and how they were "made" to feel this way or that way, which is nearly always an uncomfortable, unpleasant feeling. I politely, briefly, stop them at this point, and I relay to them that I can empathize with how they have felt, and understand the frustrations of not feeling right in their own skin. I also let them know they aren't alone; that many, including myself, have been in their shoes.

I proceed to ask them about therapy, and if there was any time in their life where they saw a therapist or a counselor. Some answer affirmatively, with most of them showing anger or disgust at the experience. Not too surprisingly, many of those had the therapy forced on them by their parents, or a spouse, because those people in their lives saw something that made them uncomfortable – whether a behavior or a presentation – and thought that psychotherapy would be the cure. A few, albeit a *very* few, have told me they had been to therapy and did have a positive experience and they go on to share with me some of the things they had learned.

More often than not, however, too many people just starting out on their journeys of transition have not seen a therapist to learn the life skills and positive coping mechanisms that are needed to live an emotionally positive life. They've come from broken places; depression, substance abuse, anorexic behaviors and a myriad of mental disorders, as well as from situations of discrimination or violence.

When my therapist let me go after a year and a half, (yes, my therapist "fired" me,) she told me she'd given me all the tools necessary to get better, but I didn't understand. I blamed her just as I'd blamed everyone before her for the horrible life I was living. I was unable to see those seeds she had planted in my heart and in my mind, because I was still full of the rage and anger of too many years of unhappiness. I was refusing to let go; to open up and see all of it for what it really was.

What I had failed to acknowledge through all those months of therapy was that I, *me alone*, was the common denominator in all the negative situations I had been blaming all those years. And that it was up to me, alone, to make changes within myself in order to heal from the hurts and the fears to which I had reacted in anger. Some of the anger was a righteous anger – such as towards the abuse my grandfather and mother had inflicted upon me – but even righteous anger needs dealt with constructively.

Over time – over months and even years – I learned to draw upon the tools my therapist had given me; and slowly, painfully, I began to heal. My anger slowly subsided, my hurts became less painful, and my reactions became healthier as I encountered normal life circumstances. I learned what "triggered" me, what set me off, what "pushed my buttons"; and I found that on almost every occasion, it wasn't the current situation, it was something from my past, something that had originally been the source of the anger or pain. I learned that my behavior in reaction to that event could be altered and the resulting consequence (outcome) could be different, even positive.

When I see fighting and rebelling against therapy, it generally tells me one is not ready to accept full responsibility for their lives, past and present. I know I wasn't ready to accept my own part which I played throughout my entire life until after I lost everything and everyone that meant anything to me.

It is my sincerest wish that the transmen and transwomen who come to me for advice listen to my story and realize that in moving forward with a successful transition means more than just the physical effects of hormones and surgeries, it's also the healthy emotional experience that goes along with it which helps to determine the ultimate success. Therapists can be life-givers if one would only give them a chance.

11

The Discrimination in Stereotyping

"We play into the definitions and stereotypes others impose on us and accept the model-minority myth, thinking it's positive, but it's a trap just like any stereotype. They put a piece of model-minority cheese between the metal jaws of their mousetrap, but we're lactose intolerant anyway! We can't even eat the cheese." ~ Eddie Huang, *Fresh Off the Boat: A Memoir*

STEREOTYPING IS a form of discrimination, even if not conscious. However, its roots contain some truths when it comes to gender. When comparing friendships – between two women, two men and between a man and a woman – certain fixed behaviors are generally exhibited.

Women tend to value talk (i.e. communication) and they form their intimate relationships from it. Women express themselves, share personal feelings, fears and problems, as well as talk about daily lives and activities. Women are each other's confidantes, and they are expressive and supportive with each other, demonstrating empathy.

Men's relationships tend to center around shared activities, especially sports, and this has been described by more than two-thirds of men in one study as more meaningful than talking (Swain 1989). Men cultivate camaraderie and are less likely to share intimate details with each other. Friendships tend to revolve around reciprocity, and instrumentality helping each other through rough times; but they are less likely to talk about feelings to other men. Men also tend to exchange slaps, punches and other playful touching rather than displaying physical intimacies such as hugging.

Friendships between men and women are a bit challenged because of undertones of sexuality and sex-segregated socialization; however, both have something unique to offer each other. For women, it's a less emotionally-intense relationship than with other women, while men find the relationships personally affirming and they're able to communicate more freely with emotion than with other men. Men generally talk more with women than with other men, but they also get more attention, response and support than they offer.

With all that said, now I want to talk about the media and how it has shaped not only our culture but those around the world. Media is a primary reason that transgender people suffer discrimination. The media influences most people's opinions, identities, choices, and lives; and people rely on and use media on a daily basis from television to radio, social media sites, magazines and newspapers. One influence of the media is that media tells us what's important by directing our attention to issues and events. There are "gatekeepers" who determine what reaches the audiences of mass media – which includes editors, owners, producers, advertisers, and even the White House.

The media often portrays women negatively and focuses more on appearance, attitudes and behaviors rather than accomplishments. The media tells men and women what they should be, should wear, should look like, and are biased in that they will portray more white men than women or minorities. Women are consistently portrayed as sex objects, passive and stereotyped.

Advertising is notorious for displaying women as the domesticated gender while men are portrayed as tough, white provider-types, and as being the stronger, more dominant gender. Books stress the importance of appearance – looking beautiful, sexy, and popular – and women are more generally portrayed as a supporting role rather than the lead role. Music videos show females as strippers, prostitutes or other sexually exploitive situations just waiting for men to pay attention to them. Men are nearly always seen as independent and capable, and usually having authority over the woman.

Even with all these social cues from media and advertising, many transgender youth challenge these binary gender stereotypes; many times beginning at a very young age. When this occurs, parent's efforts at maintaining socially acceptable behaviors escalate.

Their child might be a biological boy but his preference for dolls and pink dresses bring strong objections from the adults as well as siblings and peers. These objections might be subtly disguised, (buying toys "appropriate" for the child's gender, and so forth,) but the negative and disapproval messages are communicated, nonetheless.

In my case, it was the desire – even the need – to wear clothes I felt comfortable wearing, and playing outside in the dirt with my Tonka Toys was a joy. I was fortunate that my parents allowed me to occasionally play with such toys, unlike other gender-variant or trans kids who didn't have the same opportunity. But as I grew older, my desires to embrace the "masculine" world around me served only to make my parents uncomfortable and unwilling to participate, and they became more forceful in communicating appropriate feminine behaviors.

I was sent to a private high school where female students were required to wear dresses. The old adage "A woman's place is in the home" rang true in our household. Women who were unmarried were spinsters and teachers. Women had no role in any churches, except to oversee the bake sales or be church secretaries.

I was forced to take typing and dictation classes though; I suppose my mother thought perhaps if I did have to work, it would be as some rich man's secretary. Home Economics classes were forced upon me where I learned to cook and sew, and my chores were doing the housework, because that's what I was "supposed to learn".

I don't fault my parents for any of this, because I realize they were products of a generation that, in the 1930s-1950s, they, too, had learned from their parents the social etiquettes of femininity and masculinity. By the time I appeared in 1961, the social and culture rules were already set in place. Unfortunately, through many years of adulthood I experienced the dissatisfaction of my family because I "chose" to be different. By the time I transitioned, my family had communicated their total disgust of my "lifestyle" and disowned me. I suppose it wasn't a big loss, considering the abusive and dysfunctional relationship we had through the years.

Some of the ways members of the transgender community are subjected to stereotyping are things like the too-often-mentioned "man in a dress" and the bathroom restrictions because people don't want "men" in the ladies room. Many non-trans people (cisgender) believe that trans people are confused or mentally ill, and still others believe that trans men and women are gay. Well, they are right about some, because gender identity has nothing to do with sexual orientation – and there are heterosexual as well as homosexual transgender individuals, just as there are in the cisgender community. Some people also think that transwomen are drag queens. While it may be true that some transwomen perform on stage, they are not in "drag" since they are already women. To go further with this, not all individuals who perform "drag" are gay (or lesbian), yet the stereotype is out there and believed.

Another popular belief in society is that transgender women aren't real women, and trans men aren't real men; while others see trans people as "deceivers" – using their presentation to pretend they are something other than their biology. One author puts it like this "The stereotype derives from a contrast between gender presentation (appearance) and sexed body (concealed reality). Because gender presentation represents genital status… people who 'misalign' the two are viewed as deceivers." (Bettcher, 2007)

Some people believe that all transgender people want to change their sex, forgetting that there are plenty of those under the transgender umbrella who are perfectly happy with their bodies as they are. Transsexuals, on the other hand, *do* have the desire and need to medically transition in order to align their bodies with their affirmed gender identities.

Each of these stereotyping scenarios are the basis for much of the severe discrimination that occurs against trans people, and I believe it is up to us – not just the researchers and advocates and activists – but *each of us* individually to help educate those around us in order to dispel these potentially harmful stereotypical thought-processes. Only by ending the incorrect views, thoughts and opinions of those who don't understand transgender people will it help end the discrimination and bigotry so prevalent in society today.

12

Manning Up

"Sexism occurs when we assume that some people are less valid or natural than others because of their sex, gender, or sexuality; it occurs when we project our own expectations and assumptions about sex, gender, and sexuality onto other people, and police their behaviors accordingly; it occurs when we reduce another person to their sex, gender, or sexuality rather than seeing them as a whole, legitimate person. That is sexism. And a person is a legitimate feminist when they have made a commitment to challenging sexist double standards wherever and whenever they arise. An individual's personal style, mannerisms, identity, consensual sexual partners, and life choices simply shouldn't factor into it." ~ Julia Serano, *Excluded: Making Feminist and Queer Movements More Inclusive*

I WROTE ABOUT STEREOTYPES in the last chapter and I think now is the time to bring up this subject. I'll keep this chapter short by saying what I am motivated to say, then leave it to you to ponder for yourself.

It's a phrase I hear all too often, "manning up" and I don't believe it's a helpful phrase at all. In fact, it perpetuates the stereotyping problem in society. From what I've seen in the transgender male community, those who were first using and promoting this term came from a radical or separatist lesbian background; and, after hearing it enough, the term has spread throughout the trans-masculine community.

So many transgender and gender-variant people are advocating for the dismissal of the gender binary in society, yet I believe by using the term "manning up" for transmen, they are playing into the social and cultural stereotype of what being a man is all about and using gendered speech to reinforce it. I honestly can't see that this is helpful to newly transitioning guys and I truly believe it continues to perpetuate the gender gap and sexist philosophy in society as a whole.

For myself, I have always, *always*, just been *"me"*. I have gone through many life experiences, with two-thirds of my life living in the female role. I identified as *"me"* when asked (*"I'm just me"*) and rejected societies labels when I was put in a box. People decided who or what I was by observing the people I was (supposedly) sexually intimate with at any given time. Sometimes I was labeled a lesbian, while at other times I was labeled as wearing the proverbial "pants in the family" when I was in a relationship with a man.

When I made the decision to medically and physically transition, it was not to "become a man" (I had always been one, despite my appearance.) I did not feel like I needed to change who I was on the inside, and I did not need to "act" like a man (manning up.) I was just myself, and that meant I needed the outside – the part that people saw and judged me with – to reflect what was on the inside. I did not need to prove to myself or anyone else that I was a man, I just wanted to be comfortable inside myself with my outward appearance.

When living as a female, I never cried and I was aggressive and dominant. Now living as a male, I cry over heartwarming commercials, I am mild-mannered and I am either dominant or passive appropriate to situations, nothing to do with gender. I did not "man up." I became *myself* even more fully and deeply than I had ever been before transition. I cannot say I "feel" like a man, because I have no idea what a biological man "feels" like, I only know that I am perceived as a man, my physical appearance is one of a man, and I like myself and the person I've become.

Why do some of us reinforce the very thing we are trying so desperately to change? Using "man up" or "manning up" needs to stop. Even in our government, several States in America are beginning to recognize the harm in the use of gendered language and providing legislation to adjust words like penmanship, freshman and watchmen to handwriting, first-year students and security guards. It's been several years – I believe it was back in the Seventies – when the term "stewardess" was changed to "flight attendants". This was back in the Second Wave of the Feminist

Movements, and their fight for equality and recognition beyond the right to vote and have a quality education (First Wave) was in the forefront of society right alongside of and beyond the Civil Rights Movement with the fight for having a right to their own bodies.

Using, or not using, gendered language is something we in the trans community need to be acutely aware of in our daily communications. I realize that many things we say are so common that it's difficult to even notice. Terms like "mankind" treats men as the default, and although it was intended to include all of us, women are completely excluded from the term. Using "man" to refer to all of us establishes men as the norm against which everyone else is judged – and in this and every other sense, everyone else is women. The same goes for the term "you guys" of which I was guilty of using often enough. I realized it when I said it to a group of transwomen – and immediately apologized for the term. I even sat down with them and talked about it quite extensively, and since then I have witnessed women who adamantly reject this term around them and will be very vocal about it when it happens to be said.

Well, I have gone off on a tangent about gendered language when I have a later chapter in the book already written about changing the language of gender. I will get back on track and finish this chapter with the following words…

Any – and I stress the word *any* – words, terms or

phrases which exclude or belittle half of the human population are harmful and misogynistic and *must be removed from our vocabulary* if we hope to achieve full equality and respect for all genders.

13

Privilege – Not Just a Man's Subject

"What is this 'Privilege' I'm talking about? It's not how we act, but rather, it is how others perceive us and react to us and how it becomes beneficial to us. Privilege is when one person from a particular group can behave a certain way, and it doesn't offend anyone and it's perceived as "expected" from members of this group. But members of another group can behave the exact same way, in the exact same circumstances, and it's not okay. It's frowned on, it's ridiculed, and it's seen as defiance, or rebellion, or attention-getting." ~ *Michael Eric Brown*

SINCE I'M ON THE SUBJECT of gender and stereotypes, I think it's necessary to briefly address another aspect that I think about often – that of privilege. Privilege, to me, is suggesting that not all people are created equal. It goes right to the heart of the social and gender "boxes" that we've all been put into; the restrictions and constrictions and expectations which I have talked about and written about elsewhere (and will continue to do so.)

I named this chapter with the byline of "Not just a man's subject" for a reason. Privilege occurs and is obtained when an individual transitions to the male gender and equally, it also diminishes when an individual transitions to the female gender (where one "gains", another "loses"). So although I am speaking of *male* privilege it affects *all* of us in the trans community, and I am hoping that what I share here will make sense and become yet another set of ideas to ponder.

I have experienced the phenomena of unintended male privilege, just as many transgender men experience it. Transmen automatically achieve some level of male privilege, wanted or not, as soon as they are socially perceived as the men they are. For many, this is a positive experience, but there is also the other side of it that is not-so-positive, and it isn't something we can control.

I have heard many transmen, especially younger ones (generally under thirty years old), who, prior to physical transition or in the early stages of taking Testosterone, speak of the male privilege they either look forward to, or are already experiencing. To them, without knowing the full extent of what male privilege really means, it seems to be an exciting time for them. This wasn't something that I experienced; the want or desire to achieve male privilege never entered my mind. But much of my transition was done privately with very little personal exchange with other transgender men due to the fact that social media hadn't gained the extensive popularity it is now, and at the time information on female-to-male individuals was still very limited. (In fact, the very first time I typed "FTM" into a search engine I found two types of results returned – the first was a music group, I think, I didn't really pay attention since it wasn't what I wanted, and then plenty of porn sites came up with trans women with degrading terminology. It was difficult to find much of anything on transmen, though after a lot of digging I came up with a few websites and the organization FTM International, of which Jamison Green was a past president.)

There are, what some transmen would consider "positive" examples of male privilege. There have been various research studies over the past few years that show female-to-male individuals earn more, and/or have more raises on average than male-to-female individuals and even cisgender women doing the same work in their place of employment. Men are more likely to be waited on quicker and more efficiently than women at restaurants and other places of business. Men generally can walk alone at night and not expect to be sexually harassed and go on a date without expecting to be raped. Men are not penalized for not spending excessive amounts of money on grooming, fashion or appearance, and men can be promiscuous and not be called "sluts". These "positive" examples, however, are exactly what the term "male privilege" means, and for each positive a man experiences, a woman experiences exactly the opposite. How does this, then, become a "privilege" to aspire to for some transmen?

On another side of the "privilege" coin, however, men are expected to provide for their family, and if they choose to be homemakers while their Significant Other/Spouse earns an income, they are often immediately labeled as no good, or users or slobs. Men are expected to protect their female counterpart even going as far as physical violence, if necessary. Whereas, if a woman were to show violence to protect a man, that woman is the subject of scorn while that man is ridiculed and put to shame.

Women have privileges, too, though few ever take the time to think about it because they are wrapped up in declaring that men have male privilege, *for which I do not fault them since they are absolutely correct.* What are some of these privileges?

Women can bear children. Although men can, too, with the right anatomy (specifically, transgender men, but that's another subject for someone else's book). Women can be emotional in public including giving hugs to each other and kissing on the cheek without repercussions. Women are first off the ship, and are usually first through a door. Women are not expected to be the breadwinner, and it's acceptable for them to be a homemaker, although the economy now demands both spouses/partners to be working if one is unable to secure a higher paying job. Women are not generally seen as a threat nor as potential rapists or abusers, as opposed to men who are automatically avoided when walking alone in the dark, and sometimes even in the daylight.

As far as transgender women, it is true that there are some transwomen who exhibit residual signs of male privilege. Let me be clear – I am not saying that all transwomen do, nor that they are male or that this is a critical issue. I'm only sharing what I've observed through many years in the transgender community, and I know it is visible to others as well. It seems to occur more in transwomen who have transitioned later in life. It seems some of the learned traits, actions and behaviors of having been assigned males from birth and living in a socially acceptable male role or "position" (which I'll talk about more in a later chapter) seem to have transferred into their new societal "role" in life. I don't believe some of these women are aware of it. I think perhaps it has carried into their new lives uninvited. I'm not saying that it can't be unlearned, *nor should it need to be*. I don't find it any different or unexpected than transmen who bring some of their "female" traits and roles into their new life.

We all cry discrimination and inequality when we see that women make only seventy-seven cents for every dollar that men make, and when women are passed over time and time again for promotion and advancement in our places of employment. We proclaim injustice and inequity when we see the gender gaps in the executives of corporations and the prevalence of the male-dominated political arena. We also, finally, promote women working and allowing the men to stay home and raise the kids without too much of an ado; but with all of our outcries – and even with the cultural and societal changes we've had in America and elsewhere – we still continue to perpetuate the gender gap with our language and behaviors.

You'll find more about what I mean as you continue reading this book and how it is related to being trans and the gender roles and expectations for us and of us as men and women in today's society. For now, I just want to try to gently compel you to be aware of the harmful effects male privilege has on not only women, but on *all* genders.

I think it's imperative that transmen acquire a keen awareness of male privilege and learn to support affirmative action for women (and all genders). I wish to remind transmen that though you may be in or entering into this new world of male privilege, always remember that *where there is a "privileged" group, there has to be an "unprivileged" group.* Try to put yourself back into your "female" shoes before you lose (or refuse to accept) this truth, and try to make changes in your everyday life in social settings and workplaces towards equalizing this divide in society's views and treatment of all genders. That goes for your language as well as your behaviors.

14

Being Transgender in a Gendered World

"Instead of saying that all gender is this or all gender is that, let's recognize that the word gender has scores of meaning built into it. It's an amalgamation of bodies, identities, and life experiences, subconscious urges, sensations, and behaviors, some of which develop organically, and others which are shaped by language and culture. Instead of saying that gender is any one single thing, let's start describing it as a holistic experience." ~ Kate Bornstein, *Gender Outlaws: The Next Generation*

I'VE THOUGHT IN DEPTH about our male-centered and male-dominated culture, feminist perspectives, transgender and gender-variant individuals, gendered violence, the entire LGBT community, and more, and how they are all interrelated. I've tried to look at others in the trans community as well as within myself. I want to talk about just one thing in this chapter – being transgender/gender-variant/gender non-conforming in the world as it currently exists.

Being a trans-identified individual, (like many other trans individuals,) I have experienced my life living as two different genders, I've experienced both oppression and privilege just by being myself at any given moment of time. I have studied and worked with transgender people for several years, including studying myself, to see how we all "fit in" (we don't, really) in different social situations. Whether we were born female-bodied (assigned female at birth) or male-bodied (assigned male at birth), we have not self-identified as the gender that society has insisted we should be. Many of us undergo mental, emotional, spiritual, and medical processes and procedures to become the person we know we are inside.

Some of us are fortunate, and are able to begin our journeys at a young age with the support of our parents and professionals who are trained to help youth in their affirmed genders. Others have waited in silence and secret well into adulthood; many through marriages, children and careers before they were able to or willing to embrace their true gender. Some have experienced very little distress, harassment or violence while others have endured unimaginable situations in their paths to living authentically.

The commonality we have among us is the deep-seated knowledge that we were born into bodies that somehow did not conform to the gender we know ourselves to be, and we have each experienced the emotional trepidation of knowing that in order to be more content with ourselves we must announce the incongruities to another human being. For some, there is a profound fear of this announcement, having little doubt there will be loss of loved ones, friends, employment or other. There are those, too, who have no doubts of the acceptance they'll receive knowing their loved ones or employers or landlords are respectful and proactive in the rights and lives of all human beings.

We are a diversified community of people coming from all walks of life – spanning all races, ethnicities, national origins, ages, sexual orientations, creeds, economic conditions, familial statuses, disabilities, and every other group and category in existence. There is only one difference between us and those who are not transgender – and that is the difference of our personal gender and sex incongruities. Nothing else. We sleep, eat, read, go to school, watch television, play sports, attend church, pursue careers, pay taxes and everything else that human beings do in their lives.

Why mainstream population finds us so threatening is beyond me – except for the influence of outdated religious values set forth by leaders in years gone by as well as in current times. I am not claiming religious beliefs are a negative thing, I'm saying that the perversion of truths from ancient cultures has taken over, spreading into something other than which they were originally intended and it has created a bigoted and unreceptive mindset among contemporary believers. Our mainstream Western culture has formed over centuries of hegemonic control by (mainly) wealthy, white, and religious males who have dictated the social structures we are faced with and immersed in today.

Growing up being viewed as female gave me a firm grasp on the sexism and male dominance that men have over women. I challenged the societal norm and presented as a "butch" female, but it wasn't because I was necessarily consciously trying to fight the system but, rather, I was just trying to be myself, and be comfortable within myself (isn't that what we all want to be?)

I didn't wear dresses except when required by my parents and the private school, and I didn't wear makeup, shave my legs, or conceive a child. I was outspoken, assertive, and owned my own business. When I was around heterosexual women, I unintentionally made them uncomfortable, although I'm not sure it was because I didn't conform to their view of what a woman "should" look or act like, or whether it was because I was too "male-ish" for them. I was never a part of a "women-only" group, which was fine with me, because I did not feel as though I belonged.

On the other hand, I found that I could hang out with men, and I was more readily accepted into their group. They looked me in the eye when talking to me, slapped me on the shoulder to say "hey, how ya doin?" The interesting thing was, though I was "welcomed" into their world, it was on a more superficial level (and gendered) than I would have liked. The men still opened the door and motioned me to walk through first. They still assumed I knew nothing about repairing my vehicles, (I didn't, but I never let them know that!), so they would jump right in and do the fix for me.

Now, if you reread what I just wrote, I said that I would never let them know I really did not know anything about repairing a vehicle. I was unwittingly falling into the cultural trap of the proverbial battle of the sexes. I thought if I admitted I knew nothing about car repair, it would somehow make me less of a "man", and I'd be seen as a female (for all appearances, I *was* female), one to be controlled and dominated, both knowingly and subconsciously. That was just one of a myriad of experiences of how the dominance versus oppression issue worked in my life.

Many years later, after having physically transitioned to male, I found myself in the position of unintentional Privilege. I want to state again that I did not transition to acquire the "rights" of being a male, I did so because I didn't identify as a female. My self-identity – my gender – was male. Suddenly things changed. If my car broke down, men in the near vicinity simply went on doing whatever they were doing and they didn't offer to help. I was supposed to be able to fix my own car. I can't just drive up to AutoZone anymore and expect they will come out to change my wiper blade like they automatically did when I appeared female.

What do you think I do now when my wife and I are out and need a wiper blade? She drops me off around the corner and goes to AutoZone herself, because they will happily run out to change the blade for her, then she picks me back up when it's done.

Many transgender and gender non-conforming men and women consider themselves feminist or feminist-thinking, myself included. I think feminism with its theories and perspectives has been an important and vital voice in our society, and the movements have effected many positive changes in a relatively short amount of time (when one views the inequalities, commodification, objectification and enslavement of women historically.)

I deeply believe that anytime a change is needed that it takes the voices of many to effect the type of changes that are needed. It is my hope that I may be reaching a few hearts and minds while you're reading through my thoughts and perspectives, and that you might, too, decide to be one of those voices so that trans and gender non-conforming people will someday be able to live and walk safely and equally on this earth.

15

You're SUCH a Guy!

"What we ask is to be human individuals, however peculiar and unexpected. It is no good saying: "You are a little girl and therefore you ought to like dolls"; if the answer is, "But I don't," there is no more to be said." ~ Dorothy L. Sayers, Are Women Human? Astute and Witty Essays on the Role of Women in Society

I HAD HEARD these words in the title many times throughout my adult life when I was perceived as a female. Usually, it was immediately following some ridiculous statement (i.e. egotistical or macho) that I'd just exclaimed (usually about women.) Although I had chosen to live with women (who just happened to be lesbians,) I had also chosen not to "hang out" with many women, preferring the company of gay men. Straight men were "too" macho, and spoke of foreign interests; such as cars and sports, and bragged about their recent "conquests" with women. Gay men spoke of fine food and restaurants, heartwarming movies and, of course, Cher, Liza and Patsy (stereotypes, anyone?)

For too many years, I didn't specifically identify myself as being a male, yet I knew without a doubt I was not a female. I'm not sure what I thought I was, but if someone asked me how I identified (which happened often enough), as I've said earlier, I always answered *"I'm just me"*. If the few lesbian acquaintances pressed the issue, my answer was "I'm just what you see – nothing more, nothing less. If you want to see me as a butch lesbian, that's your right".

They did call me a "butch", or "dyke" or sometimes androgynous or "studly". They definitely never called me a "femme", as I was not - not in *any* sense of the word. I wore men's clothes, or tailored women's jackets and a more feminine-colored shirt when necessary for employment, rationalizing to myself that "gay men wore pastel shirts," so therefore, it was acceptable for *me* to wear pastel.

What made them call me a guy? Sometimes, it was after they asked me how many people I'd been intimate with. I admit, I lost count somewhere along the way by the time I was thirty years old. Maybe it was because I felt there were *some* jobs that females weren't physically or emotionally capable of performing (I've since changed my views.) Perhaps it was due to the way I dressed in male clothing, or the fact that I preferred hanging out with the guys rather than with the lesbian *cliques.*

One thing I knew – I was emotionally different than the female species. I didn't cry at movies (stereotyping again, I know,) and I was angry, loud and often. I made derogatory comments when I saw a woman doing something in a movie that I felt was just plain idiotic (running to the basement with no way out when being chased by a killer,) and I couldn't understand at all why women needed to be "aware" and "alert" when walking alone at night, preferring to be in the company of at least one other person, and always having their car keys poised in their fist to ward off an attacker. I had none of these fears, and I was unable to understand why they had so much of it.

The picture above paints me as a misogynist pig, I know. I suppose, in a way, I was. I had no time for women's emotional outbursts, fashion, makeup, babies, etc., and avoided groups of women like they were the enemy out to castrate me. Some probably would've tried just that if I'd had the appropriate parts in my pants. I preferred to live with women as they were more "tolerable" than heterosexual men, and gay men didn't offer me the opportunity or understanding for a close relationship at that time whether as lovers, or even simply as roommates. So, I learned to "hide" most of my thoughts and opinions on men and women, knowing I'd be the brunt of angry outbursts and forced social isolation if I said how I really felt.

Truth, self-actualization, and acceptance all came in the matter of a few moments during one of my therapy sessions. I had once again made some ridiculous remark that I don't remember now, due to whatever my therapist had just said, and she just shook her head and (yes, I swear) rolled her eyes. Coming from her, the words "You're SUCH a guy!" hit me like the proverbial two-by-four.

"Maybe that's because I AM a guy," I proclaimed defiantly (and secretly, even proudly). There, it was out in the open. Reality set in, and from that moment forward, I knew exactly who I was, what had been "wrong" my entire life, and where I had to go from that point forward.

Almost as quickly as the realization of my self-identity surfaced, so did my sexist way of thinking begin to dissipate, albeit slowly. The more I focused on being *"me"* a guy, even though continuing in a female body at the time, the more I saw changes in the way my social groups treated me.

I began researching the subjects of gender, and gender transition. I searched for and read as many blogs and social network postings written by transgender men and women about being transgender, gendering, misgendering, discrimination, and societal expectations. There wasn't as much information out there on transgender men when I first started my search; I am thankful there is so much out there now for those who are just starting out.

I began seeing in a social context the pros and cons of being a woman as well as the pros and cons of being a man, and I began to not only rethink my sexist views of women, and stereotyped views of both men and women, but I also began to change those views without much effort, as I was finally living authentically.

As I began my physical and medical transition a

few years later and the testosterone began to take its effect on me, society in general began treating me differently. Where once my hairy legs and armpits offended people in general because I appeared 'female', it became acceptable as a man to have this hair. Where once I would be ignored or dismissed or given barely a glance at a checkout counter or restaurant, I soon found that I was receiving attention, even flirting, from the employees.

What happened to me, and what happens to many transgender men, is that darned "male privilege", and for me, it took this social phenomena to turn me into an all-gender-loving person instead of the male-chauvinist jerk that I had been previously. So once in a while there is some good that comes out of being a guy!

16

Living Authentically

"Instead of being presented with stereotypes by age, sex, color, class, or religion, children must have the opportunity to learn that within each range, some people are loathsome and some are delightful." ~ *Margaret Mead*

A LONG WITH the popular question of "When did you decide to become a boy" come the questions of a similar nature... "How long have you known?" and "When did you decide to change?"

I take these questions in stride now, realizing it's an opportunity to educate. However, it did take me a long time to have answers, because deep inside myself, I was churning with various emotions trying to answer these questions as honestly as I could.

For many transgender people, the right answers are *"I've always known"* or *"Since I was very young,"* and *"As soon as I found a doctor to help me."* But my answers are not that simple, and those answers don't really give the people the answer they are really seeking, which is the need to understand. What I believe they're asking is, rather *"How did you know?"* and *"Why did you feel it was important to medically transition?"*

Have I always known I was a transgender guy – did I know when I was little or even as an adult? Of course not. Back then, the word "transsexual" was a little understood term, seemingly reserved for a couple of well-known people in the news, and "transgender" was not to be born until the late 1960s.

So in looking at the question even deeper, did I know I was a boy? In all honesty, no, I can't say that I did. Did I know I was different? Yes, absolutely. Did I know at three years old that I hated dresses? Yes. Did I know I preferred Tonka trucks over Barbie's? Yes, of course. But these "facets" of me, these definite feelings and preferences did not surface at that time as a deep conscious thought (even though I had that penis I wrote of in an earlier chapter!)

As I wrote in the last chapter, for much of my adult life people would tell me, usually in shock or disgust after I'd make some sort of unfiltered comment, "You're SUCH a guy," and I inwardly smiled at this comment. Little did my therapist know that when she made the statement, it finally hit home with me. It was the old cliché of the "light bulb" going off in my brain. A guy? Yes! *Exactly.*

From that moment on, I began to live authentically. I was mentally accepting of the fact that I was, indeed, a man, not a woman. I immediately began using a male name (a variation of my female name that evolved further into what it is now.) Eventually, it followed that I would pursue a physical transition, though not for several years. Once I accepted myself for who I was, life was easier to live; and through the next few years I worked on my past hurts and traumas, began to heal and then I began to enjoy the little things life has to offer. Once I'd gotten that far, and my medical issues had subsided enough, I knew it was okay for me to physically and medically transition.

Here I am, a transman. Transsexual? Yes. Transgender? Yes, for me I am under that umbrella term. But I rarely call myself either of these. I am just a guy, or when needed for educational purposes, I'm a transman.

I recognize that there are as many definitions of self as there are selves, and there are those who don't identify as transgender. Or transsexual. Or perhaps they identify as both. The one thing most of us have in common, however, is that we were not comfortable with who we once *were*, and have chosen to begin living authentically as the person we *are*.

All we can do is be that person we are – and become the *delightful* rather than the *loathsome* that so many in society still view us as being.

17

Sometimes I feel like a Man... or Not

"As it turns out, we're all still learning to be men, or women, all still learning to be ourselves." ~ Jennifer Finney Boylan, *She's Not There: A Life in Two Genders*

DON'T GET ME WRONG, I am a man. I'm not physically "male" as science or medicine would determine, but my *mind* is male; my *identity* is male. For all intents and purposes, I am a man; both personally identified and defined as well as socially in appearance and behavior since transition.

Speaking or thinking in semantics – what is a man? What is a woman? What does it mean when someone says "*I feel like a man inside*" or "*I feel like a woman inside*"? How can I – a female-bodied person at birth raised as a girl in a typical female role – really know what it means to *feel* like a man?

Do I identify as one? Yes. Do I Think like one? Yes. Do I look like one? Now I do. But what does it really mean to "feel" like one, though? I have met so many transgender people who say "*I have always felt like a man*" or "*I've always felt like a woman.*"

I was brought up and raised as a girl and was taught typically "girl" things. I was subjected to the dreaded start of menstruation, grew breasts at an appropriate age even though I (first thought I had one, then…) had prayed diligently for a penis. I was forced to wear dresses because that's what girls do. I was taught how to apply makeup and promptly decided I could do without that. I had to wear a shirt around people (then at puberty, a bra, too) because that was appropriate for a female.

I know the "feelings"; those "emotions" evoked from being raised this way. I know pain, and anger, sadness, guilt, and other feelings, but I'm not sure that the terms "man" or "woman" can be defined as a *feeling*. If they can, then what exactly *are* those feelings?

I *feel* like a man in that I *identify* as a man, I think much like one, (most of the time anyway,) I look like one (thanks to Testosterone!) I sound like one (again, thanks to the wonder drug, although I personally think I sound more like a teenage boy than a full-grown man in his fifties.) I used to have the libido of a man, (again, I'm a man in his fifties, it eventually slows down, trust me.) Like a large percentage of men, and nearly all teenage boys, if it moved and breathed (or even if it didn't breath,) it was a potential sex partner.

I act like a man, or rather, like what's socially expected of a man. I open doors for women allowing them to walk in ahead of me, and I offer my seat when a woman is standing and there are no seats left. I take care of the finances at home and I plan the logistics of vacations. I also fail to read instruction manuals, and I try never to ask for directions. Fortunately, my smartphone helps me with navigation now, so I'm not lost near as much as I was prior to owning it! I typically lose track of important dates, and like any self-respecting gentleman, I call Road Service when I get a flat tire (oh, perhaps that's the old "female" in me, not wanting to get my hands dirty?)

On the other hand, I have also done most of the cooking and housework in my relationships, (until my current one,) which is typically a woman's job. I can iron pretty darn well if I have to, but sending the clothes to the dry cleaners is so much easier. Now I don't even worry about wrinkles, I'm in shorts most of the time and I don't have to worry about dressing up for work. I used to send several "I love you" and "Miss you" texts to my wife throughout the day when she was at work, (she is retired now,) again a typical female thing to do, and I was sometimes temperamental when she didn't respond back as quickly as I wanted her to. I get teary-eyed over television programs, (and sometimes commercials!) though I would *never* let anyone see this side of me. I get up to get the tissues to hand to my wife who is also teary-eyed, and this gives me time to compose myself before handing them to her and possibly being seen.

Honestly, for myself, I'm not entirely sure what it means to *"feel like a man"*. I wasn't born one or raised one and although I *am* one and live as one and am recognized as one, all I can truly say for sure is:

I feel like me, and whether male or female, man or woman, typical or atypical, I don't want to change me, or worry about what people think of me, or what roles I might take in the whole gender identity spectrum.

Being me, however – and it's a situation that many trans people find themselves in before, during and after transition – is facing the question *"Where do I fit in?"*

I never relished hanging out with the women at family functions. I wasn't interested in hearing about sewing, cooking, what their kids were doing, or fashion talk. But that's where I was expected to be, so that's where I was. As I mentioned previously, once I was an adult, I mostly hung out with gay men.

I now have the opportunity and for the expectation of others to "hang out with the guys", (whether straight or gay) and what do I do? I tend to stick with the women at my wife's family functions, as well as in group functions, unless there happens to be other transmen, in which case I will always "hang out" with them. I can't relate to the (generally heterosexual) men's talk about sports, cars and construction work. I couldn't care less about a carburetor; much less know what one looks like.

I was reading through an article on the Art of Manliness website one day which talked about how to "feel like a man". I thought I'd share two of the suggestions I found there which I believe could also be transposed into how to "feel like a woman" for transwomen. I think the suggestions I'm sharing here are words of wisdom for just about any human being.

The author suggests things like "Figure out what sort of man you want to be" and "Start doing the things that sort of man would do." (Brett, 2012) He continues that last bit of advice with "Even if you don't feel like it" but I don't necessarily agree with him about this. I believe we should all do what we feel is right for us at any given time.

I agree, however, that we as trans men and women all need to decide what kind of person we wish to be – what kind of person do we wish to present to the world – then work towards that goal of being just that person. *Nothing more and nothing less than being the authentic person we are.* Doing the things men or women would do? Yes, to a certain extent, I believe so, because society and cultures have expectations of men and women and if we are to live as men and women, we must follow some of the rituals that go with our gender. I don't mean conformity without individualism – this takes away from our freedom to just "*be*" who we are.

As a "for instance" to explain why I say the above… if you're a woman you will naturally use the women's bathroom (to the dismay of many right-wingers) and vice versa if you're a man. If you're a woman, you more than likely will keep your legs closer together when sitting and wearing a dress. If you're a man, you'll be more apt to give up your seat to an elderly person entering the bus or the room. I think these are just social "graces" that come with the territory of a male/female world. Societies and cultures are changing, albeit incredibly slow – but with the voices of the gender-variant in the world, many past social expectations of appearance and behavior are no longer quite the binary edicts they once were.

Changing the tone a bit, I was reading another article lately which was talking about violence in prison settings. It spoke of the punishment and degradation that men experience in prison (and, in my opinion, in life outside of prison) and how they are "*made to feel like women*". The author wrote,

> It is as unnatural and wrong for women to be degraded, dehumanized, and sexualized under coercive circumstances as it is for men to be" [and goes on to explain that his article] "suggests that examining the sexual abuse of men in prisons can help disrupt the persistent and uncritical linking of feminization and women....[and] expose the artificiality and violence of compelled feminization (Franks, 2004).

The point of his article that I deduced after reading it was that when men are made to feel like a woman it is "an insult to basic dignity", and that failing to recognize the harm of imposed femininity is in the nature of imposed femininity itself (the social script that exploits physical vulnerability.)

My own take on this is that when men or women have socially defined roles and positions imposed upon them, it serves only to perpetuate gender violence. I say to this – step out of the discriminatory socially imposed roles we have been given while still holding true to our affirmed genders. There's a fine line, I agree, but there *is* a line. One that allows us to *feel* like the man or woman we are, and the one that society tells us we must adhere to. I will cover more about gender roles and positions in a later chapter, but for now I will leave it with one last (extended) comment...

Our perception of ourselves – and how we *feel* in our gender – sets the tone for how others perceive us. This is true regarding things other than gender, too, such as when we *feel* depressed, others respond to us in certain ways due to our actions and behaviors. When we *feel* like a man, or *feel* like a woman – we are just *feeling* like the person we are. I believe others tend to behave accordingly in most instances because our gender exudes from our being. The reactions aren't always what we wish, because society hasn't been thoroughly enlightened or evolved far enough away from binary thinking, but I think you'll find that, in general, many people will simply take you as you are and how you behave as a *person* (not specifically *acting* like a man or woman) will set the tone of their own behaviors.

If you *feel* like a man, then great! If you *feel* like a

woman, then equally great! If you *feel* like neither, then that is great, too! As long as you *feel* authentic and comfortable in your gender and *in your person*, then that is all anyone can ask or expect. Life is what it is, and for trans men and women – being a man or a woman or an androgynous, gender-less being is the foundation of life and the catalyst for future changes in social ideology as we strive to simply *be ourselves* in the world.

18

There's Lint in my Belly Button

"A good laugh overcomes more difficulties and dissipates more dark clouds than any other one thing." ~ *Laura Ingalls Wilder*

JUST TO ADD a bit more humor, especially after talking about feeling like a man, or not, and before I delve more deeply into social roles and positions, I thought I'd share more of the lighthearted aspects of transitioning, something that trans guys might find fun to read. The following is a blog posting I wrote several years ago after being on Testosterone a few years. It generated many comments and I have subsequently removed the online version of this in favor of including it here.

Laugh all you want but, it's true! I have finally figured out WHY after all these years of not having this problem, and now it's here. I first noticed it about a year into transition. Imagine my surprise – I had never had lint in my belly button, but now I do. It dawned on me that it's due to one of the most cherished aspects of taking testosterone – hair!

Yes, those darned stomach hairs. I remember being so excited when they first appeared; even more so as they became longer and darker and it no longer looked like peach fuzz. They looked like real MAN hairs!

I had always wondered why many/most of the men I knew through the years had belly button lint, because I didn't, nor did the women I lived with seem to have it. Now I know that it's because most of the men have stomach hairs and, of course, the hair traps all sorts of interesting particles and then forms this annoying anomaly called "Belly Button Lint".

Speaking of hairs – how about these facial hairs, guys? Almost every transman I know has a lifelong envy of their dads, their brothers, uncles, and male friends and the rite of passage in life known as "shaving". We pick up a razor and try it out in secret – long before transition – just to "pretend" we have this particular male quality. Some continue this strange and unnecessary ritual for years for nothing else but to *feel* like the man they know they are. Some do it in hopes that the little bit of peach fuzz might grow out darker and thicker the next time it shows. It doesn't, but we keep hoping and shaving.

Then the day comes when we finally start our Testosterone. The excitement builds. The anticipation grows almost unbearable as we look in the mirror every day, several times a day, waiting for those first MAN hairs to appear. It drives us crazy. All we can think about is hair! (Well, that's not quite true – food and sex are right up there with hair.)

The day comes when we wake up and run to the mirror, and there is indeed a new crop of what looks like it might be a bit more than "peach fuzz". Oh, the excitement! We grab the phone, we run to the computer, we wake up our friends who are sleeping in on their day off, and tell them, "I've got a mustache! I've got a mustache!" or, "I've got 4 chin hairs!" We celebrate, we rejoice.

We continue in our excitement, unable to stop talking about all the new facial hair we see each day, each week. We drive our friends utterly crazy to the point that they no longer want to be around us, because all we talk about is HAIR. (I'm sorry, Lillian!)

Finally, after a few months of having a mustache, even the growth of a genuine beard, we settle down, and begin to seriously look at how we are going to take care of this new addition to our face. Do we shave? Do we want a goatee? Do we just want sideburns, and some "stubble?" Thus begins another few months of deep concentration on our facial hair grooming habits. And even more talk about hair.

Finally, we wake up one day and walk in to the bathroom to shower and shave, and realize that having facial hair is much more work than we **really** anticipated. We love it, now don't get me wrong. But now we remember the days when we just walked in, took our shower, dried off, and got dressed and didn't have that darned extra step called "Shaving" and grooming our face that we now have for the remainder of our lives. There's the expense of razors, (and usually more expensive ones, because facial hair is thicker than other – and women's – body hair,) and shaving cream and aftershave, and for those with beards, the expense of a trimmer. And the time involved on a daily/several times a week process to keep ourselves looking semi-respectable. (This is not forgetting that, yes, as "women" most had to shave legs or underarms, but we as transmen forget the hassle and societies expectations of that as we look forward to our facial hair that is not scrutinized like leg hairs on a woman. Besides, if a woman doesn't shave, she can hide that fact with clothing. Men can't hide their face.)

Oh, and don't forget the nose hairs. Wow. Whodathunkit? Facial hair, body hair - all cool. But this nose hair is really something totally unexpected in the whole scheme of things. I won't even get into the care and maintenance of nose hairs, I'll leave it to your imaginations.

Would we change it or do we regret taking T? A vehement "NO!" But trust me, to all of you pre-T guys – shaving's not all it's cracked up to be.

But enjoy it, because it is somehow a part of acquiring that darned "male privilege", and it's who we are. It's not privilege in the traditional feminist sense, but it is a privilege nonetheless. Think about it – I mentioned society's views on women and leg hairs, but as men we don't encounter this same critical analysis that women endure. We can wear just about anything and any colors we want (plaid shorts and striped shirts together!) and very few people give us a second glance;

we can have a beard or not have a beard and it won't even enter the minds of those we encounter in our day-to-day lives. Men's appearance has never been the primary target of the fashion and media industries like women's appearances. Sexualizing and objectifying men seems quite low on their radar.

19

When Our Brains Are "Socially Constricted"

"I suppose it's not a social norm, and not a manly thing to do — to feel, discuss feelings. So that's what I'm giving the finger to. Social norms and stuff...what good are social norms, really? I think all they do is project a limited and harmful image of people. It thus impedes a broader social acceptance of what someone, or a group of people, might actually be like." ~ Jess C. Scott, *New Order*

IT SEEMS TO BE a never-ending issue, the "bathroom" debate, so it stands to reason that I decided to write about it and share my personal experience with public bathrooms. Around the year 2010, I found myself needing to finally make a public comment on the issue of bathroom usage after reading a blog post one day. Here is the gist of the blog post which is followed by my experience after more thinking and pondering about the comment I made.

The writer of the blog post was making a point that if you're presenting as a woman you should use a women's restroom and vice versa regardless of your physical sex. The writer went on to write that sex segregation of restrooms is a matter of social convention, not law, and that the solution is simply that the American public needs to "get over" their hang-ups". At that time, the bathroom issue in courts hadn't come up yet in Arizona where I was living at the time. Also, remember that gender neutral bathrooms weren't as common in most of the U.S., even just a few years ago, as they are becoming now.

Just days prior to reading the comment I was at a transgender conference in California on a small university campus. The bathrooms were marked *Gender Neutral* and each had more than one stall. I spoke about this experience I am going to share with you now to some of my friends who were with me at the time. I've since thought about it quite deeply, as I realized more and more the impact this situation had on me. The following is my personal introspective look at the situation that followed.

I've been using male bathrooms since my transition, as well as prior to transition when the women's restroom was full (*"When ya gotta go, ya gotta go!"* was my motto.) I had never had the occasion to use a "gender neutral" bathroom until the conference since they weren't all that prevalent yet, although I had heard of them and thought to myself that this was a viable solution to the "bathroom issue". I had even been actively promoting the use of them for the transgender community. I realized later, however, that until one has actually experienced a situation, one cannot necessarily make an "informed decision" about how they *feel* about it. (Yes, there's that word again –

feel). Now, don't jump to conclusions about what I mean by this until you hear me out.

When I walked in to the "gender neutral" bathroom a transwoman followed close behind me. This particular bathroom was equipped with 3 stalls. I chose the stall on the end. She chose the one beside me. Keep in mind that I knew this woman both as a friend as well as professionally.

Now, I happen to be one of those men that sits down to pee. I'm usually conscious of this fact when using the men's room in public places, as are many transmen. (As a quick note here, to those who are first starting out – it really does get easier and it's not the big deal you imagine it to be if you'd just stop worrying about it.)

Though it's none of my freakin' business, I happened to notice that she sits down to pee, too. Why this would be something I consciously noticed, I'm not sure, except that it must have been my subconscious coming to the forefront. If I had not seen her come in with me, and she had simply entered after I was already in the stall, I have to admit that I would have not thought much about it, except for the fact that I may have mentally noted on some subconscious level that 1) she sat down and 2) she had women's shoes on, therefore, she was the "opposite" gender of me. It would not have come up as a conscious thought.

As I sat there taking care of my business, I realized I was feeling and thinking *something*. I wasn't sure what the *something* was, just that it was something out of the norm of general thoughts. I tried to analyze the feelings, but was unable to define them in any sort of rational way. Once we were on our way out of the bathroom, we both commented to each other on the "oddity" of the situation. It was her first time, also, using a gender neutral bathroom. Neither of us could explain our own feelings about it.

A few other people I had known up to that point and others I've spoken to since then admitted having similar thoughts and feelings the first time they had used a gender neutral bathroom. All are thankful to have the opportunity, all are thankful these bathrooms exist in some areas, and all are thankful they didn't have to experience being uncomfortable because they had to wait or use a gendered bathroom. Yet each of the few I've spoken with agreed that the first time, even subsequent times, prompted a *feeling* unlike any other.

Socially, we have all become accustomed to either "male" or "female" constrictions with bathroom use. We aren't at all prepared to mentally wrap our brains around peeing in a public stall next to the "opposite" gender. We're not used to walking into a bathroom where there's a line of both men and women waiting to get into a stall or wash our hands afterward while seeing both genders at the sinks beside us. I imagine it's easier and less "odd" for the younger generation, especially in light of the many gender non-binary and gender-variant individuals coming out into mainstream society.

Funny, though, we do it in our private lives with our families and our spouses. Many of us grew up with brothers and sisters, and peeing with the bathroom door open was not uncommon. Running in to brush our teeth while another family member was in the shower didn't bother us.

At what point did social constrictions take over and dig their way so deeply into our brains, that some of us as transgender people find this becomes an "odd" situation sharing a bathroom with men and women, even ones like ourselves? Why was it even a situation for me to create mental notes? I'm almost appalled at myself, and am ashamed that I felt that feeling of "oddity" in the situation.

Most transgender people experience the same fears – those same uncomfortable feelings when we first began transition and were faced with starting to use the "opposite" bathroom of the one we had always used. We all know how strange it felt to walk into these small public spaces amongst our peers and share the intimacies of peeing next to each other.

We have no idea what's in the pants or under the skirt of the person in the stall next to us despite what gender they present or express. Who really cares? We're all in the bathroom for the exact same reason – to eliminate. Period. It's a normal, human function.

I had to reevaluate and redistribute my own way of thinking and looking at this issue. I realize I had to "get over" my own "social constrictions" that had been built over a lifetime of indoctrination, and realize that we are all "just human." Why should I care who is peeing next to me? After all, I'm only in there a couple of minutes, it's not a social situation, and we all have to do it. I have come to the conclusion that I still believe "gender neutral" bathrooms should become the "norm".

I believe the writer of the blog comment was right – American's need to get over their hang-ups. I believe that we, as transgender and gender non-conforming people, need to help them do it. I believe, although it will take time, that educating the general public as well as even some people in the transgender community, is something imperative and a "must do" in order to break down these "socially constrictive barriers" to living our lives comfortably and safely.

Social constrictions suck. Society says we are wrong for living outside the box. Society says we must blend in to be accepted. I say...give social constrictions the finger as the writer of the beginning quote has done.

20

Do Social Circles Mean Separation?

"For human beings there is no essential femaleness or maleness, femininity or masculinity, womanhood or manhood, but once gender is ascribed, the social order constructs and holds individuals to strongly gendered norms and expectations." ~ J. Lorber, *Paradoxes of Gender*

WE ALL GROW UP being taught what is socially acceptable for our gender and what our roles are in life. It becomes apparent early in school where the boys hang out with boys and the girls hang out with the girls. The boys talk about sports, and cars and of course, girls. The girls talk about makeup, hair styles, shoes, or clothes, and of course, boys. Young boys have belching contests and young girls giggle when talking about some new teen idol, or squeal with excitement when a popular boy winks at them.

As we get older this behavior continues as the men hang around the water cooler at work and talk about sports, and cars, and about their wives or girlfriends. The women gather around the lunch table and talk about hairstyles, or a new pair of shoes, or what her husband or boyfriend did or did not do the previous day. Many men still belch loudly and many young (and sometimes older) women still giggle uncontrollably when noticed by a good-looking guy.

We feel comfortable around people of "like" gender. We feel like we belong and feel a sense of solidarity and camaraderie. We have separated into groups that make us feel comfortable. At least, we're supposed to feel this way.

When we're transgender growing up, (whether we have defined it at that time or not,) we don't necessarily feel this way. We feel out of place, like we don't belong with the other women or the other men. We try to fit in but, more often than not, we are unable to do so comfortably.

Eventually, the day comes when we figure out what the problem is. That "problem" is, simply, we *aren't like* other women, or we *aren't like* other men. We aren't, because that's not necessarily our "gender". We are transgender.

We then embark along the wonderful journey of transition. We find others who have walked this path before us and we talk to them and we learn. We find support groups and social get-togethers. And guess what we do? Yep, you guessed it. We continue to separate ourselves from the "other" gender.

If you attend a typical gathering of transmen and transwomen, you'll almost certainly find the men hanging out with the men, and the women hanging out with the other women. Only now, the men aren't necessarily talking about sports and cars, more often than not they are comparing their hair growth, talking about acne medicine, or how big certain body parts have grown or sharing the excitement when a man's shirt fits them properly for the first time after a surgery. The women, however, are more stereotypical and on any given occasion you can find them talking about shoes, hairstyles, and makeup tips and the cute guy at the grocery store who winked at them. No, people, I'm not making this up. I've been to dozens and dozens of gatherings of transgender men and women, and have personally witnessed this over and over.

Society has placed conditions on all of us, whether we are a transgender person or we are comfortable in our biological assigned sex. The "conditions" are the socially acceptable rules of behavior, and we as transgender men and women are not immune. We, whether consciously or unconsciously, follow these behaviors before and right on through to after our transitions. These rules manifest themselves all around us, especially in the media. Through the ages, the media has defined society; the good, and the not so good.

Movies and television shows teach us what it means to look and act like a woman or how to be a "real" man. We're taught how to dress, what is sexy, and what is not. We are taught standards, and, if we don't follow these standards, we're ostracized, and criticized, or people simply laugh at us. On the sadly not-so-subtle side of it all, they discriminate with blatant hatred, or worse, commit violence against us.

If a boy wants to wear pink, he's called a sissy or gay. If a girl wears a flannel shirt and jeans, she's called a dyke. Society and media have twisted sexual orientation and gender identity, blending them together and creating labels. When we don't conform, we are outcasts and labeled freaks and worse. Society and the media has taught us how to dress, how to act, and how to interact with others. It has taught us that women talk about certain things and men talk about certain other things.

Are we as trans men and women much different than people who aren't transgender? In the context of social gatherings, going strictly from what I've witnessed for several years, we really aren't much different. With the exception that we have all been on the "other" side, and have a greater understanding of both genders and are much more open to blending together to share our common experiences. (Getting us to "blend" in a co-ed group isn't as easy as it sounds, however, but that in itself is typical and another subject.)

I am a man in every respect, but I still choose to hang out with the women at my wife's family functions in heterosexual situations. I'm not comfortable around the straight guys. I don't feel as though I fit in, and rightly so. I didn't grow up a boy, I didn't have the same experiences as boys do, so I am completely unable to relate in a close social situation to the conversations men have when gathering in a group situation. In transgender functions, however, I tend to hang out with other transmen rather than the women. Why? Because I am just not interested in shoes, clothing and makeup – I never have been interested in these things, so why would I be now? I assume the women are completely fed up having to hear about our beards and hair growth, too, so really it's understandable why we segregate ourselves.

What's wrong with once again breaking out of the box? That's exactly what I do when I choose to sit beside my wife in the group of women relatives. I may be bored to tears, but it's still more comfortable to me than out with the macho-ness, competiveness, and egos.

So how and why do these obvious separations exist? As toddlers, we play with others our age without much, if any, regard to gender. We all play with the toys we're given, we fight and share and for all intents and purposes enjoy our social time together. We don't know anything different since time has not fully defined our social roles at this point, though we've already been subjected to varying degrees of gendered social cues that have begun to creep into our innocent brains. Eliot says "Parents are never really neutral about gender. Regardless of which toys or clothes we buy them, we cannot help but react in different ways to our sons and daughters – if only because of our own long experience of 'male' and 'female'" (Eliot, 2012, p.

2). So from the first moment we gaze into our parent's faces, we are experiencing gender cues in the ways and manners in which they return our gazes.

Girls and boys display distinct differences in expressions and responses within a few weeks to a few months of their arrival into the world and although some of this can be attributed to biology, much of it has to do with the behavior, presentation and language of the people and objects around them. For instance, with certain studies on sex differences in infants "researchers studying the newborns have to be very careful to remove (or have others hide) all gender cues in the hospital room so that they do not unintentionally bias babies' behavior" (Eliot, p. 73).

I point out this evidence of the effects of gender cues because as I've always believed and spoken about previously, our schooling on what makes a man and what makes a woman begin from the moment of birth (and possibly before birth, if one subscribes to the theory that a fetus hears and absorbs the outside world from within the confines of the womb) – and this education, unintentional as most of it has been, has determined our present behaviors in and about peer groups throughout our lives.

Isn't it time we begin educating future parents, medical personnel, and educators on the power and effect their own socially-defined gender behaviors, thoughts and language has on children? One big-name corporation recently took a chance and stepped outside the box by removing gender labels in their stores and I say – it's about time! Public reaction has been mixed, with many people expressing anger at this bold move, but the fact remains this is just one step in the right direction to removing the socially-ingrained gender rules we've been forced to live with.

This is just one way to begin changing society and how we all relate to one another as men and women, girls and boys. Perhaps one day it will be common to find co-ed groups where people of all genders are interacting and mingling together with conversations that are inclusive of all.

21

Challenging My Position

"I'm just tired of people judging me because I fit into a certain mold." ~ Gillian Flynn, *Gone Girl*

IN THE LAST CHAPTER, I wrote about a major corporation who took the initiative to begin changing gender perceptions and norms. I give them kudos and respect for this incredible task of challenging society's positions on gender. I wrote the following a few years ago when I was thinking about challenging the system as we know it, and it seems appropriate to share it here.

Thoughts of different people I've met during the last few years are drifting to the front of my mind. Thoughts of a friend who married another friend of mine, and of one who recently published his own book, selling copies the first day it was out. Another one left the State to return to the dismal surroundings of her previous life, while yet another is sleeping on the streets because he isn't ready to face his addiction to Methamphetamine. There's the one who went back to school in his mid-to-later sixties, now in his early seventies and getting closer to graduation; and the one who was eighteen, excited at high school graduation because he was graduating as a young man with his chosen name and the beginnings of his brand new life living his dream. One who spends most of his waking moments working even when he's not at his job, cell phone in hand, while another sleeps as much as she can when not at work to avoid having to face her day-to-day life. Another left his home country in Europe to explore the freedoms of America, but finding out his comfort zone was really back home in Europe, he returned to his life there.

All of these people I've mentioned, including myself, have something in common. Not overlooking the fact that our lives are very much like anyone else's on this planet, we each have a very special parallel to each other. Each of us began our lives being told we were something we were not. Arriving abruptly from our mother's wombs, we were assigned a "Position" in life, one that didn't fit our own sense of rightness. It was a declaration the doctors made upon seeing our physical bodies. More specifically, it was a decision they made upon seeing our genitals.

This decision, based solely upon those hidden places that only a few people see for the rest of our lives, has impacted *every single thing about us* for the rest of our lives. Some of us realized it early in life during our formative years, and we spoke up loudly hoping someone would hear us. Some of us experienced the discomfort of knowing something was amiss, but were unable to define it until we were much older, and we kept this distressing "anomaly" hidden from others, yes, even sometimes from ourselves.

The "Position" I write about goes deeper than the words "It's a Boy!" or "It's a Girl!" The "Position" these others placed us in is a universally defined, culturally accepted, religiously mandated, socially acceptable status in life. It's a place where others make judgments about us based on their own limited visual and mental perceptions. It's a pre-defined Box with sides and a top and a bottom, and there's nowhere we should be except "inside the Box".

One of my acquaintances is 6'2" in height. She towers above my own lowly stature of 5'3". She wears a wig, as her own hairline has receded. She's spent thousands of dollars having unwanted facial hair removed, while I look in the mirror wishing my beard would fill in the rest of the way (which it won't, it has "done-did" its filling in, but I suppose it's good enough!) She's one I could call upon when I need something "manly" done, such as lifting a heavy box or moving some furniture (there's that gendered language, again!)

Another person is close to my height; wears men's boxers, and men's jeans and shirts. His voice is female, though he's had testosterone swarming through his body for several months. He is adamant about using facial washes and creams, knows how to apply makeup, and it doesn't bother him that this is typically a "female" behavior.

Again, all of these people were assigned a "Position". Most of them, as well as myself, have since made the decision to alter our "Position", and live truly and authentically as who we really are. We live outside the conventional "Box" we were placed in early in life. Not all choose to physically transition, but each chooses to live as their true self, whether it is being a man sporting facial cream instead of a football, or a woman who prefers watching football over chick flicks.

When I lived according to my "Position", I wore dresses, because that's what was expected of me. I took ballet lessons and played with Barbie dolls. That is, I did this until I screamed and cried and demanded that I play with the Tonka trucks and GI Joes, and I pursued learning how to survive outdoors with only a multi-function knife. I was still expected to learn how to bake pies, and follow when dancing, and why shaving my legs was a "must do", instead of a choice. I chose not to shave them, which immediately put me at a great disadvantage in my "Position".

Because I was non-conforming, (as well as having my outrageous attitudes and behavior,) my school and my parents believed I must have a mental disorder, and treated me accordingly by forcing me to see numerous doctors, therapists, psychiatrists and psychologists. I was forced to take medications that would either "cure" me or "control" me. As I wrote in an early chapter, I spent those years overly medicated, switching from one kind to the other when one wasn't working with no weaning off of one before moving on to the next. (Withdrawals, anyone?)

My "Position" kept me in a constant struggle to fit in; into everywhere I went and in everything I tried to do. I was expected to find a man, marry and have children. I was taught typing, and shorthand, and was expected to read Emily Post to learn proper etiquette. I was told to keep quiet, not state my opinions, and to swoon over babies. I was expected to stay with the women in the kitchen, and not lounge around the TV with the men during the holidays. I could play volleyball, but not football, softball but not baseball, and only kittens, not frogs, were to be played with. The color pink permeated my bedroom, from the chenille bedspread to the curtains and the throw rugs. Blue, or brown, or any other color, was unacceptable. I was told I could not speak in church, as it was not something someone in my "Position" could do.

I was told by my grandfather that my "Position" was beside him and underneath him nearly every summer for eighteen years, and that it was also my "Position" to keep it our Secret. I was told by my mother who said while under the influence of her opiate-based drugs that my rebellion would turn me into a recluse like Howard Hughes; that I'd grow long fingernails, be anemic and anti-social, and I'd eventually end up going to Hell. She couldn't fathom or understand that I was already there, in my own hell.

I grew older and entered the vast space in time

called "adulthood" and found out that the "Position" was even stricter; it was brutally enforced, daily, by all who surrounded me. I was expected to take jobs that were "appropriate" for women, and forget being able to pursue a carpentry career, or a maintenance position, or construction. If I were to join the military, I would be expected to wear skirts and uncomfortable women's dress shoes, rather than the smart-looking uniforms the men were allowed (expected) to wear.

I did try to live somewhat according to the "Position" of expectations held over me, so I married a young man I had known in high school. Very quickly, I found that being a "wife" was not for me, and we divorced. At the same time I left home to get married, which was a week or so after high school Graduation, I had immediately ceased to take all the prescribed medications, being positive I wouldn't need them anymore since I was leaving the source of my emotional troubles.

However, having been on so many drugs for so many years, I found there was an addiction, though I didn't know it at that time. This propelled me into taking street drugs within those first days of leaving my parent's home. After a year and a half of taking everything I could find to fight my "Position", as well as drinking to drown my emotional pain, and pimping my body and my belongings to fund my habits, I realized it was time to come clean and stay clean. I went on to do just that, and followed the long path of learning to live without drugs. I will talk more about addictions and self-harming behaviors in a later chapter, because I believe these "Positions" I'm speaking of here have a lot of influence on our coping behaviors.

At the time of becoming sober, my rebellion against my "Position" became even more clear and noticeable. I was choosing, however, to live as *me* with only my own expectations of myself being what mattered to me. I chose to wear men's clothing and cut my hair short, and there would still be no shaving of my legs, or my underarms.

Summers and wearing shorts and tank tops brought grief from strangers as well as from people I knew and cared about, as they let me know not only verbally, but with their obvious looks of disgust that I was an embarrassment to all those in my "Position". Cashiers didn't bother to take a second look at me, deciding quietly that I was not "normal", and grunted their "thanks" for my patronage. Law enforcement spent extra time scrutinizing my looks and spent time visually exploring the insides of my car from through the windows during routine traffic stops. Food Servers appeared to force themselves to take my order, not looking me in the eyes and gruffly answering any questions I might have when they weren't able to switch tables with one of the other Servers.

I found a "community" where I felt like I semi-belonged. I became enamored by a young woman at the halfway/recovery house I was living in at the time I stopped using drugs. She introduced me to a group of lesbian friends and, for a while, I felt like this might be where I should be. Very quickly I realized I didn't fit with them, either. But the community-at-large – the entire LGBT community – seemed to accept me as I was, hairy legs and all. They didn't judge me, or have any expectations of me, except for me to be true and honest with myself and with them. I ran into issues with lesbians, however, because I didn't conform to their ideas of what a lesbian should be and do. That's another story for another book.

Through the next few years, I stayed in this community, and did my best to get by in the "otherworld", the world that wasn't LGBT-friendly. I found a career by accident simply by owning a computer. When the rest of the world was just realizing there were computers small enough to sit on a desk in their home, I became an expert, having learned to program and build them, and how to repair them when they quit working.

Soon, I was "wanted", because I had a skill that few others around me had. I spent years repairing computers, eventually opening my own store to do this because I loved doing it. I left the LGBT community temporarily when the "otherworld" accepted me and overlooked my appearance to take advantage of my skills. I was finally in a "Position" that was acceptable to me, and appeared to be so for others. Or so I thought.

Over the years, the novelty of being the "female" computer expert wore off, and the fun of the competition with this "man's" occupation wore thin. My discomfort with my life, and my "Position" became obvious through the next several relationships with women, and a second marriage to yet another man, followed by a prompt divorce.

As the popularity of being a computer technician grew, people tended to choose the male computer-geeks over this oddly-dressed hairy woman, perhaps because they thought a man knew more than I, a mere female. Perhaps because they were more comfortable around someone, a man, who believed their "Position" was an asset and a privilege. Perhaps my being non-conforming wasn't so great. After all, I was still expected to have a husband, wear dresses and makeup, and have a few kids I was raising. Then they could claim I was a "forward-thinking woman", one who could manage a full household, and hold an esteemed career at the same time.

By this time, I'd held a career in the computer field for nearly seventeen years, subsidizing during the rough times with odd jobs, mostly manual labor, as I had no other skills or education to fall back on. I began teaching computer systems networking at the college level.

A year later, I was standing in front of a classroom of thirty students, and I suddenly felt like I was out of place, I was lost, and I was incapable of going on. I walked out of the classroom in the middle of my lecture and went directly to the only thing I knew which could help me forget what I'd been avoiding my entire life – alcohol.

Three weeks later, with no memory of where I'd been, who I'd been with, or how I arrived home safely, I made two calls. One was to a treatment center 450 miles away, the other to request a sabbatical from my teaching position. I made it thirty days into the treatment before my anger and fighting forced them to let me go.

To expand on what I wrote in an earlier chapter about my anger and therapy, I had been assigned a therapist at the treatment center, and she agreed to continue seeing me outside of the center. Although as I wrote earlier, she fired me after an intensive year and a half, she told me I had the potential of getting better, but as long as I fought her, fought life, and fought society, I was not going to heal.

I was devastated, and within a month I had lost everything, including all of my friends because of my anger. After living in my car for a few weeks, someone took me in on their couch, and I slowly began to apply the lessons I had learned from my therapist. For the following two years, I spent every day learning about myself and about the world around me. I learned to live in the moment, as the Buddha taught. I learned how to make amends, as the 12-step groups I attended had taught me. I learned how to recognize and release the lifetime of anger I had been carrying. I learned how to allow my other deeply hidden emotions rise to the surface, and I learned how to forgive myself, and how to forgive others. I learned how to be thankful for each day I woke up, and how to enjoy what I had, instead of wanting for more.

The most important thing I learned, however, was that it was okay to be *me*. It was okay to accept and to embrace the fact that I simply wasn't going to ever fit in the "Position" I was assigned to at birth. I was told to be a woman, but, in fact, I knew I was a man. I didn't need to live as a woman, I could live as the man I knew I was, and I could live in society with a contentment I couldn't possibly have dreamed existed.

Many years later I was living a whole new life, married, and in a new "Position". After having taken Testosterone and having surgery that took away the uncomfortable double Ds that had been such a telltale sign of my former "Position", I was able to look in the mirror and see who I really was, knowing others saw who I really was, and I liked it. I liked it a lot. I liked how I looked, I liked how my life was going, and most of all, I liked how society accepted me just the way I was, in my new "Position".

Here in this "Position" I find the good as well as the not-so-good. Cashiers smile at me now, and talk about the weather, or other mindless subjects. Food Servers are light-hearted and helpful, and both the young men and women working at Starbucks flirt with me. People pay attention to me now, and listen to what I have to say, even when it's not important. I can have my hair short, and not shave my legs, and people still respect me. I can wear a tie and get compliments instead of snubs, like "women shouldn't wear ties". People totally understand why I wouldn't want to carry a baby in my womb, and are thrilled at my ability to show emotion and my inability to be macho.

On the not-so-good side of this "Position", I discover that little children move away from me now to behind their mother's legs, because I'm a strange man. Women walk on the other side of the street or take another aisle in the store, to avoid this man they see before them. Law enforcement sees me in my old clunker vehicles, and again, they look me over thoroughly to make sure I'm not a threat. I can now be accused of sexual harassment or be seen as a predator. People have expectations that I can now lift heavy objects or that I can change my own oil in my cars. Just for the record, I have never changed a tire, I have always carried Road Service for that, or gotten help from someone else (men, of course.) And I have never changed my oil either, nor a spark plug or a wire, although I do manage to pour in a fuel treatment additive into the gas tank when I fill up my old clunkers.

The friends I wrote of earlier are like me. They come from many backgrounds, religions, cultures, and experiences; and they all spent a greater portion of their life trying to conform to their assigned "Positions". They each found they were unable to do so and be happy and content. They each, like me, broke free from the expectations of society and proudly made their journeys into the men and women they are today. Others see me, and them, and find the inspiration and the courage to begin their own journeys.

Each of us who are transgender carries with us a Gift. It is a Gift of having lived as both genders, and having the experiences to share, and to educate, and enlighten others on what this means to us. It is the Gift of understanding; of both sexes, of society and perceptions and expectations. It is the Gift of being able to choose to live authentically in a world full of people trying to be who they are not. Each of us has experienced the Special Moment when we were able to proclaim proudly "I'm a Girl," or "I'm a Boy," despite what the doctors said in the beginning. We each have the Gift of being able to look at ourselves in the mirror and knowing we are exactly who we are supposed to be, and that our own happiness is preferable to a life of misery, depression and self-harm due to trying to conform to who we are not. And we are alive, and well, and we are everywhere.

22

Sisters. Husband and Wife?

"I believe that the imagination is the passport we create to take us into the real world. I believe the imagination is another phrase for what is most uniquely us." ~ John Guare, *Six Degrees of Separation*

I COULD HAVE titled this chapter "Gender Roles" but it would not have grabbed your attention in the same way, would it? Previously I mentioned the game my sister and I played for years, "John and Julie." I bring it up again, because I believe it touches on not only gender identity issues, but also the "roles" or "positions" which are forced on us, or those we react to in an opposite way of what's expected of us.

My sister was adopted into our family three plus years after I had been brought into the household. I remember that afternoon moment in which I met her very clearly. I had been out with our neighbors, an elderly couple who lived across the graveled country road from our house. I suppose they would be considered my "godparents", but my adoptive mother was very conservative religious, and using the word "god" for anything other than her own "Heavenly Father" would have been, of course, sacrilegious.

Ed and Elizabeth were from England, and had

come to the States following after their son who had come over for college and had decided to stay and become a U.S. citizen.

I had been placed in their care often, when my mother needed a break. I grew to love them over the 11 years they were in my life, and looked forward to the respite when I was sent over to their house for a few hours. I have many fond memories of spending time with them, and cherish the love and patience they bestowed on me.

But continuing my story (I do get sidetracked, don't I?) Ed was driving, and his wife Elizabeth was in the passenger seat. I was standing on the back seat of the four-door sedan. As we drew near to my house, I saw my parent's car in the driveway. I began jumping up and down on the seat, hitting my head in the process, and shouting *"They're home! They're home!"* I knew I had a new baby sister in the house, and I couldn't wait to get in there to see her.

Ed parked the car, and I jumped out. I ran into the house straight into the room I knew was going to be my sister's room. My mom was there, sitting in a chair in the corner near the crib, holding my sister and a bottle of milk. I stood in awe at the little thing in front of me, and quietly with reverence asked *"Can I hold her?"* My mother answered *"No"*, and gave no explanation, completely ignoring my subsequent pleas.

I don't remember if I ever did get to hold her, but I will always remember the sadness I felt when I was told I could not. It didn't stop me from loving her, though, and I was as devoted to her as a big sister could be.

She, like any other child, began to grow and soon we played together as most sisters would, of course. She had the girl dolls, and I had the boy dolls. I somehow felt I needed to protect her, that it was my role in our lives, and I was her constant companion through the next few years. We were inseparable.

Remember I talked about the game we played early on? The one in which we escaped our mother by morphing into our alternate selves… a married couple, named John and Julie. As I mentioned, I was John, of course, the husband. The Protector. And Julie was my wife, the love of my life, who depended on me to fight off the dragons and the demons who were determined to slay us.

We sailed the vast oceans on our ship, (my bed) and flew over the rainforests, deserts and valleys (up high on a branch in our big Elm tree). We explored many caverns looking for hidden treasures, fighting flying creatures, poisonous snakes and gigantic spiders (in the neighbor's dilapidated old barn full of bats, harmless garter snakes and granddaddy long-legs.) We spent hours escaping into our fantasy worlds, finding one adventure after another to keep us occupied and away from the realities of our home life.

In reality, I knew it was my mother and grandfather who were the "dragons" or the "demons" I was protecting Julie from, but I'm not sure Julie knew that until she was several years older. I took the punishments when they were doled out, I would always take the blame, even if it had been Julie who had done something wrong.

I would also make sure I kept our grandfather away from her, by substituting myself in her place with him. He only tried once with her, and she told our mother. When I was confronted as to whether it had ever happened to me, I lied and said no. I think I did so for a couple of reasons. First, I knew he would be very upset with me if I had told (duh, right?) and secondly, I think I somehow thought that in allowing it to go on, him abusing me, then he would stay away from my sister. It was a child's logic.

When I look back and think about why I assumed the male/protector role, or even why we created a male/female dynamic in our games, the answer comes easy. It wasn't necessarily a conscious thought in my mind as a child, that I identified as male, I just knew it felt right, so in what I thought was pretending, was really giving me the opportunity to express my real self. Just another way I was challenging my position.

23

Society and the Realities of "Blending In"

"Bodies are not only biological phenomena but also complex social creations onto which meanings have been variously composed and imposed according to time and space." ~ Katrina Karkazis, *Fixing Sex: Intersex, Medical Authority, and Lived Experience*

A FRIEND OF MINE and I were engaged once in an email conversation which evolved into a discussion about trans people not being able to easily "blend" into society. My friend is a male-to-female transgender woman (MTF) and I am going to summarize some of what she wrote, followed by my own personal thoughts and my response to her:

She wrote about how she wanted to walk the earth and not be judged. She wanted to be able to walk into a restaurant or a bar or a party or work and just be a woman. She didn't want second glances, she didn't want people looking at her thinking she was a woman with a penis. She didn't have a problem with openly talking about being transgender if someone asked, but she just wanted to be treated like other women.

She continued, next talking about relationships, saying she felt that men, and lesbians, are phobic – they may say it's okay, but they are worried about what their own friends might think. She's afraid that she may spend her life alone. She felt that any time she walked into a public place, people would look at her, know she was a transwoman, and she'd know her "cover was blown."

I thought about what she said and tried to imagine how she felt. Being a transman, I "blend in" and, unless I tell people I was born a female, they generally have no idea. The thought never enters their mind. After much thinking about it, I responded to her email and I'm sharing here my response to her. It may not be the response everyone agrees with, but then again, it's mine, I own it and it's the best way I can relate at this time.

An African American man comes in to the sports bar and sits down with you and begins a conversation. Without a conscious thought, you begin talking to him. But you see it; his skin is black. You can't help it, it's visible. But it doesn't affect your conversation, your perception, or how you treat him. You don't think twice about it; you treat him as a human being.

Even forty or fifty years ago this would not have been the case. Society and laws made it difficult, and in many areas illegal, due to the bigotry and preconceived notions about African American people. Because of people standing up for the rights and equality of blacks, America slowly changed over time and it's rarely a concern in someone's mind now, except for the minority of close-minded, bigoted people who have refused to change their way of thinking. We now have had a black President which couldn't have happened even ten to fifteen years ago.

We, as transgender people, are now coming to the forefront. We are visible in society. The words "transgender" and "transsexual" are slowly becoming household words, mostly due to the positive media reinforcement and educational shows. Behind the scenes, the ones who educate society as well as the media are the advocates and activists. These are the ones who aren't always visible outside of the transgender world, they are the ones who are standing up for our rights and for our equality, the right to be seen and treated fairly just as any other human being.

Until some future time, many *will* be seen as transgender and/or transsexual, and people will not only notice but say something about it, or think something about it. They will be cautious, or afraid, or hateful. Because that's just the way it is right now, like it or not.

In the meantime, all we can do is walk proudly into the restaurants, the churches, the bars, and various other places of business and be prepared to educate those around us. We must acknowledge their fears and respond with kindness and show them that we are people, human beings just like them. It is our responsibility (because they've made it so) to teach them so they can learn not to judge.

My friend had also written, "*relationships are hard when everyone knows you're transgender.*" I know that she is saying that it is difficult to find and begin a relationship, rather than the obvious "relationships are hard", because all relationships are hard, no matter what gender identity and sexual orientation one is.

Yes, it's true that it's more difficult for transgender people to find a loving, accepting partner, simply because we are transgender. Speaking in generalities, straight men want biological women. Lesbians have their own issues about transgender people and will rarely fall for a transgender woman, although it does happen. Many continue to accuse transgender men of "betraying" them, (which is a subject best left for my next book.) For transmen who like men and identify as gay, it's very difficult to find a gay man that wants a relationship with a man who has female genitalia. And so on goes the list of obstacles.

Our difficulties lie not only with the way society views us as transgender men and women, but also on the fact that every person has their own sexual identity. We all have preferences as to what genitalia we prefer, or what other body features, or smells, or voices that attract us. We all have an innate desire to have a partner who has commonalities with us, from life experiences to relationship experiences. We don't always choose who we fall in love with, but there are unmistakable traits and qualities which draw us towards another person, and light that fire in our hearts.

Interracial marriages are becoming more and more common, mostly due to societal acceptance. But this is, and always will be, a minority. Speaking in generalities, most people connect with other people within their same race and nationality. The same is true when it comes to mixing religions; people tend to be attracted to someone who has something, such as beliefs, in common with them.

As time goes on, and we continue to stand up for our rights and equality, we will become more and more accepted. Some day we will walk into the restaurant or the church and sit down next to someone, and although the differences may be apparent, neither will give a second thought to it, because it's no longer an issue.

But I do believe the "problem" of finding a relationship with someone will be there much longer, and will always be harder than it is for the rest of society, because attractions and relationships between transgender people and those who aren't transgender will always be difficult to begin. This isn't a bad thing, it is just something we have to accept and live within the constraints of human preferences. The only way we are going to change society to get to the point of trans people not being an issue is to stand up and be proud, and fight for our rights and equality.

24

Depression in the Transgender Population

"Social anxiety results from being around people who are resolutely opposed to who you are." ~ *Stefan Molyneux*

WITH CELEBRITIES and well-known public figures coming out as a transgender individuals there have been hundreds of responses regarding them on social media websites. Some are positive reflections on their bravery, while others remind us that this person was not the first and we should remember each of them from Christine Jorgenson to Renée Richards, Billy Tipton to Virginia Prince, Alexis Arquette to Janet Mock, Laverne Cox, Caitlyn Jenner and Chaz Bono among others, and we need to celebrate all of them. Others are focused more on the hidden voices who have helped to advance the rights of the transgender community – those who have worked tirelessly year in and year out as individuals or within grassroots organizations to ultimately change societal laws and perceptions of the community.

Countless others, however, have voiced only negative reactions to these individuals coming out, and it is those people who need to not only understand what life is like being transgender, but also how society's negative reactions, harassment and micro aggressions affect this community.

There are many published articles and statistics which highlight the inferior and flawed medical, psychological and societal "treatments" that transgender people endure. It is no wonder that a large number of transgender men, women and youth have been diagnosed with, and have received psychiatric care for, major depressive disorders.

The *symptoms* of depressive disorders in a transgender person are not significantly different from those who are not transgender, (i.e. fatigue, weight changes, sleep issues, feelings of worthlessness, etc.). However, it can be concluded from multiple research findings that the *cause* of the depression in transgender individuals could likely be a *symptom or result of society's views and treatment of transgender individuals.*

Society's views of "treatment" for these individuals is evidenced in the number of hate crimes, bullying, abuse, denial of housing, employment, and essential medical services, among other negative occurrences. As an example, the TVT Project documented 1,123 reported killings of transgender people in 57 countries worldwide from January 1, 2008 to December 31, 2012 (Trans Respect Versus Transphobia Worldwide, 2013).

Politics, legislation, medical professionals and the media are major contributors of the societal views on various mental disorders, including depression which ultimately affect the medical and mental treatments offered to the transgender population.

With transgender youth also being more in the media focus, it's imperative to understand what many youth have to endure in families who refuse to accept their true gender identity, even after the family has seen signs of depression and suicidal behavior in them.

As youth, many transgender individuals are denied self-expression (i.e. boys prohibited from playing with dolls, or girls forced to wear dresses, etc.). Parents, educators, medical providers and religious leaders all attempt to "force" these youth to conform to what they perceive as "normal" and "natural". This creates tremendous inner conflicts within the youth as he or she continues into adulthood, if not addressed properly. *"There is far more distress induced by childhood histories of parental disapproval and punishment of cross-gender behavior than distress over their eventual adult gender identification"* (Jones & Hill, 2008, italics mine).

In addition to currently accepted treatments (medications, and/or psychotherapy), transgender youth are often forced into receiving psychiatric treatments, including inappropriate medications, ECT and involuntary commitment to "cure" them of their gender issues, rather than addressing the true causes of their depression.

This further reinforces to transgender individuals of all ages that mental health providers, society, and even themselves are flawed systems; therefore, all are perceived by the individual as just another "cause" of their depression, and they feel their pathways to care

are limited. Because of this, many transgender men and women avoid getting treatment for their depressive symptoms for just this reason.

One publication from The Massachusetts Transgender Political Coalition suggests "Transgender people may be less likely to seek treatment for depression, fearing that their gender issues will be assumed to be the cause of their symptoms, and that they will be judged negatively" (Original author unknown; quoted by several publications).

History has shown us over and over that when enough people get fed up with the negative and unequal treatment of certain groups of people, members of the human race become an enormous force in the face of these inequalities, and change occurs.

Statistics have shown us that 41% of transgender people have reported attempting suicide compared to 1.6% of the general population, with higher rates in those who experienced job loss due to bias, harassment/bullying, low income, or victims of physical assault (Grant, et al. 2009). Are these numbers not indicative of a need for a major kick-in-the-pants change of mindset towards the transgender population?

It is time for our society to step up and acknowledge how negative views, unfair laws, and continuing discrimination significantly affect transgender people. It is time for a substantial attitude adjustment in order to benefit the lives of all humankind as a whole, instead of picking and choosing who is worthy and who is not.

25

Self-Harm and Addiction

"Help, I have done it again / I have been here many times before / Hurt myself again today / And the worst part is / There's no one else to blame." ~ Sia, *Breathe Me*

IT'S NOT AN enjoyable subject to think about. In fact, for those who don't engage in self-harming activities, it's one you'd rather ignore or perhaps think to yourself *"I don't know anyone who does it, so I really don't need to be worried about it."* Perhaps it's true you don't know anyone; but then again, it's not something people do to get attention, they aren't likely to tell you and they may be engaging in it and you might never know.

The statistics are all over the place on just how prevalent self-harm is, sometimes called self-mutilation, in society. I think if anyone does an internet search on the term "statistics self-harm" or similar, they'll find the same studies and websites that I found and can do the math. A Canadian trans youth health survey presented their *"Being Safe, Being Me"* findings in 2015 showing about two-thirds of transgender youth ages 14-25 had engaged in self-injury during the past year, with a similar number of them having considered suicide. More than one-third had attempted suicide (Veale, et al., 2015). When I averaged out the numbers from all other studies I found, I think one would be safe to say at least twenty percent of youth and young adults engage in some form of it at least once in their lifetime, and it can and does continue into older adulthood for many of them.

I say "at least", because many statistics come from reports of Emergency Room visits, (and this would be a very low percentage of those who harm themselves,) and the others come from self-reporting in surveys. Most self-injurers are very private about their activity, and either will not respond to a survey or will not be completely honest in a survey. One can only speculate about the actual percentage of people who engage in self-harming behaviors.

When I talk about self-harm, I'm referring to the act of purposely harming oneself. It can also be called, as I wrote earlier, self-mutilation, as well as self-abuse or self-injury. There are many different reasons people cause harm to themselves, and as a coping strategy sometimes it's the only way they are able to cope with the stress of negative life events. Others may engage in self-injurious behavior because it takes their mind off their overwhelming emotion.

There are some who are unable to experience emotions due to traumatic experiences, and the act of self-injury triggers the production of natural endorphins that lead to a sense of pleasure; others have trouble identifying or labeling their emotions, or they were taught not to show negative emotions. Self-injury is an outlet they feel will allow them to express these negative emotions in a way that doesn't harm others or bring negative consequences from others.

One other common reason people engage in self-injurious behavior is that it is a means of self-punishment. In many instances, they have grown up in homes being told they're defective or useless, and they often feel shame, insignificance and like their life is a mistake. When I mention shame that transgender people feel, I don't mean the shame that stems from the guilt of having actually *done* something. This shame is a *reaction* to other people's criticism, an acute personal humiliation at our failure to live up to our obligations and the expectations others have of us.

There are many different types of self-injurious behaviors. Some of the most common are cutting, sticking objects into the skin, banging one's head against a hard surface, burning, pulling out hair, skin picking or pulling off scabs, swallowing poison, hitting oneself and breaking bones. Many times this behavior goes along with a mental disorder such as major depressive disorder, PTSD, anxiety disorders eating disorders and substance abuse.

Like other troubled youth, I turned to the only "solution" I knew to help me through the pain and anguish I was going through with my mother and grandfather. I began finding ways to hurt myself, physically, that no one would be able to discover. My most-often-used method was that of sticking myself with straight pins right up to the head of the pin. Sometimes I would have several in my upper arms or thighs, many times the heads against my skin would form a pattern, such as a frowning face or a skull and cross-bones. On some level, in the mind of a youth, I felt the best way I could deal with the feelings my family induced in me was to feel the sensations of the pins in my body and revel in the "artwork" they produced.

When I was eleven or twelve, my family was on our yearly vacation to the east coast to visit my grandparents, a time I dreaded each year because I knew my grandfather would be having his way with me the whole few weeks to a month or more. On this trip, we went to Kitty Hawk, South Carolina, and it was then that I saw the Wright Brother's plane and I decided to build one of their model kits. My parents, delighted I wanted to do something other than read books, bought it for me.

What they didn't know was that the airplane glue was my other "escape" from the sick reality of my life. Sniffing glue and pin "art" were the hobbies of my choice until the day I left home. The feeling of euphoria with the glue, and the release I felt from the pain of the pins was what, I believe, kept me from ending my life, although those thoughts were on my mind constantly. I felt the only way I could cope with my feelings of sadness, self-loathing, emptiness, guilt and rage was to retreat into my self-harming mechanisms for dealing with it all.

When I left my childhood home, I left those coping mechanisms behind, only to dive right into other injurious habits of illegal drugs and alcohol. After a couple of years being high on every drug I was able to get my hands on, I realized I could no longer cope with any part of my life while being high, and I sought help to stop using drugs. I continued to pacify my emotional pain with alcohol, however, for many years, to live with the inner turmoil of not only my childhood anguish, but also with the gnawing and growing inner confusion I was experiencing with my sexuality, gender expression and society's expectations of my assumed gender role and "position."

For too many years, my life consisted of numbing my pain through the use of alcohol. By the time I was in my thirties, I had also found another way of coping, and I began cutting myself. Between the effects of the alcohol and the relief I felt from cutting, I thought I was finally in charge of my life. The cutting became less until only the alcohol and 70-80 hour work weeks was enough to keep me going.

Then the day came in my late thirties when I walked off my teaching job at a college in California. I walked right out of the classroom in the middle of giving a lecture and right into the following three weeks of having no recollection of where I'd been or what I'd done. When I became conscious enough to realize my life was out of control, and after hearing from others the appalling situations I'd been involved in during those three weeks, I checked myself into the treatment center.

As I've already written, I spent the next year and a half in therapy where I learned about emotions, behaviors and coping mechanisms. I learned that in order to heal I would have to actually work at it, and that meant stopping the negative behaviors and coping mechanisms I'd been using and replacing them with constructive behaviors. It also meant I had to face my deep-seated emotions, those I had buried beneath the extreme anger I had been carrying around for so many years. Back came all the desire to harm myself, and I dove right back into cutting because sticking pins in myself seemed too childish. Funny, the things we think when we are emotionally and mentally in pain.

I remember my therapist handing me a printout of faces depicting all the different human emotions and asking me which of those emotions I was feeling at that moment. It never failed, as many times as she handed it to me in those first months; my anger flared, my finger slammed down on the page at the angry face, and I said angrily "That one!"

It was over a year before I was able to point at different faces; sadness and fear. By then I had finally learned (well, I accepted there were) different ways to cope with my emotions than cutting. I had lapses, however, and resorted back to it when I felt I'd lost control, like when I ended up homeless sleeping in my car because my roommates couldn't deal with my anger.

Slowly, but surely, I took the tools my therapist gave me and, little by little, emotion by emotion, I learned to feel a range of emotions that I doubt I had ever experienced in my life, and I acquired positive coping mechanisms that didn't involve cutting or harming myself in any way.

Starbucks had a lot to do with my healing. Really. I replaced my cutting and alcohol addictions with one for coffee, and I was at the local Starbucks nearly every day. One day I walked in and saw one of their new posters, an empty swing up in the air with the phrase "*Freedom to let go*". That phrase affected me more than just about any other in my life up until that point, and after begging the barista along with whatever cash I had in my wallet at the time, I walked out of the store with that poster. It hung on my wall for the next few years reminding me that it was okay to feel, and okay to let those emotions come in and go back out without needing to react with a negative behavior.

Don't get me wrong, I still have a temper, and blurt things out in anger, but it's short-lived and over within moments. For myself, simply walking away from whatever the situation just for a minute or two usually gives me time to cope with whatever the situation may be in a constructive, positive manner instead of running to a bottle or a razor blade as I had for so long. I don't even think about either anymore because I acknowledge my emotions, and I concede that life really isn't "all about me", that things will happen as they happen and I can't always control them. That's life. And life, overall, is good.

For those who do find the act of cutting or other types of self-harm as a way to keep your emotions in check, you are not alone. You do, however, need to find someone to talk to about those emotions, or lack of emotions. There are so many constructive ways of coping with life's circumstances, negative people, your living conditions or whatever it is that you are experiencing, and harming yourself is not one of them.

I know cutting or burning yourself, or whatever form of self-harm you're doing feels like it works. I know you think it is taking away your pain or releasing your anxieties, or even making sure you feel something. You know without me even saying it that it's only temporary, I don't have to tell you this. Because if it were a sure-fire method of dealing with life, you wouldn't continue to do it because your life would be better and there would be no more need to injure yourself. You know in your heart that it's not right, yet you don't know how to stop. Or even if you really want to stop because maybe it gives you a sense of pleasure, it is perhaps the only pleasure you can find in your life. There really are ways to cope with whatever it is you're dealing with without harming yourself.

I *could* just say find someone to talk to, but I know

you've heard that before, and you don't feel like there's anyone you'd trust. So my other suggestions would be simpler things you can do for yourself instead of injuring yourself. Try deep breathing, call a friend, and try not to be alone. If those don't work, here's a few other suggestions. Try one, try several. Don't give up if it doesn't work the first time, or the second. In fact, don't give up trying any of these suggestions because at some point, you'll find that you have made it through those feelings, or lack of feelings, or whatever it is that made you feel you had to harm yourself.

- Listen to music (think relaxing music, not death metal)
- Go for a walk
- Write in a journal (yes, it really does work, and no one needs to read it but you.)
- Take a hot bath or shower, or hold some ice cubes in your hands
- If you are feeling aggressive, punch a pillow
- Get some Play-Doh or clay and work with it. Mold it, squish it, destroy it, then do it again.
- Allow yourself to cry.

And now, back to what I said I *could* say – talk to someone. Find a counselor or therapist who you feel comfortable with, and work with him or her to learn to cope with whatever is going on in your life. Learn from them how to live your life healthy and free from self-harm. It won't be easy, but it can and will happen that someday you'll look back and see how far you've come.

26

The Language of Gender

"Once you label me you negate me." ~ *Søren Kierkegaard*

A LIVING LANGUAGE is an evolving one, but can we really change our language to change the deeply imbedded conceptions of gender? I believe we can, and here is why.

Language is a symbol and is formed within cultures. Cultures all over the world have denoted the binary – male and female – as the standard symbols for gender, although it really has less to do with gender than it does with sex. When people think of or see a penis they think "male." When they see breasts they think "female." Penises and breasts are symbols we use to classify the sex of a person. This has nothing to do with their gender – and this is what needs to be changed in contemporary thought and teachings.

What happens when an individual is transgender? Because of ingrained binary thinking a person who sees a transwoman may think "a man in a dress". Why? Because they immediately have the cultural notion that the person has (or had) a penis. Again, this is a matter of biology and sex, not a classification of gender.

There are a few cultures that see transgender people as having a gender all of their own, the Hijra, the Mahu's, Kathoeys, Two-Spirited peoples and others to name a few. In those non-Western cultures they may, for instance, immediately think of something "spiritual" rather than thinking about biological sex, even going so far as seeing the phenomena as something to be revered. This is prompted by the same *symbols*, yet the classification of male and female isn't the resulting thought. The difference is simply the *cultural* symbols and, subsequently, the values we place on gender.

One of the most prominent symbols we use to denote male and female are the signs on public bathroom doors. However, the current trend shows that many college campuses and larger corporations as well as some smaller businesses are changing to gender-neutral bathrooms.

Standard forms (documents) that once asked for a person's sex (male/female) now have a transgender or "other" option, or these designations have been eliminated entirely. Parents are now refraining from dressing their children in the common pink and blues, and are switching to colors that do not symbolize "sex", and are allowing their children to play with toys of their choosing, rather than deciding what is appropriate for their child. Look at the word "transgender". It didn't exist before Virginia Prince used it in in the late Sixties. Now it is becoming more popular globally in the media and in households. The term "cisgender" didn't come about until the mid-90's, and is finally becoming more widely used. "Bear" used to be only a four-legged hairy animal, or as a verb such as a support (the wall needs strengthened to bear the weight of the roof.) Now it is used as a term for a ruggedly masculine gay man (generally heavier and sporting more hair – much like the animal where the term stems from).

I could go on with many words that have been created, changed, added to or deleted from our language. These examples support my theory that our language can, does, and will continue to change.

Why are the gender neutral symbols and behaviors occurring? Because people are finally beginning to recognize that "sex is what's between the legs, and gender is what's between the ears" (Credit: This has been quoted by too many people to acknowledge just one person).

Society is ever-so-slowly changing their language – those symbols used to designate gender. In doing so, it is changing the very foundation of future gender roles, and, in time will reduce the gender inequalities so prevalent in all of society.

I do believe we can change our language. It will likely take decades, but perhaps with enough people, institutions, and governmental influences purposely making these changes, children being born in this decade will see the transformation in their lifetimes. And to have this happen – we continue to need both those in the media as well as those behind the scenes working towards helping society achieve full acceptance and equality for all genders. And we each need to do our part by removing gendered language from our everyday communications.

27

Only By Seeking the Truth

"The most important kind of freedom is to be what you really are. You trade in your reality for a role. You trade in your sense for an act. You give up your ability to feel, and in exchange, put on a mask. There can't be any large-scale revolution until there's a personal revolution, on an individual level. It's got to happen inside first." ~ *Jim Morrison*

A S I COME to the end of the book, I have to ask (because I'm always thinking and pondering and philosophizing,) is our self-identity really all about gender? Are transsexuals – those who choose to have hormonal and medical assistance to be able to live as the "other" gender – really just still playing into the stereotypical roles of male and female *because* of cultural and society values?

What about people who consider themselves "gender fluid", or "androgynous"? Where do they fit on the balance scales of socially constructed gender? These, and so many other questions, are topics of my current and future studies, research, and books on the transgender population.

I believe a shift in consciousness is necessary in order to evolve beyond misogyny and male-dominated society – which each ultimately affect the lives of transgender individuals and create the gendered oppression that they as well as all women experience. One strategy to interrupt the sexist oppression around us is one I employ often and I teach others to do the same. I will preface it with an excerpt from the book *The Gender Knot*:

"Because people make systems happen, then people can also make systems happen differently. And when systems happen differently, the consequences are different as well" (Johnson, 2007).

Johnson goes on to say that systems shape people's behavior, but when a person defies that system, it can unsettle other's perceptions of what is or isn't socially acceptable. The next time the others are in a similar situation, they may shift their responses or beliefs because of the increased risk of social resistance.

Because I believe social interaction, (language and symbols) is at the heart of any culture, (much to the chagrin of Functionalists and Conflict Theorists,) I believe it is the foundation of all other sociological perspectives. I advocate for people to step out of the neat little comfortable "Box" that society has put them into and speak up for those oppressed – whether it be women or transgender individuals, or an ethnic population or other.

By speaking out, it can shake other's perceptions. Keeping quiet when a sexist or racist joke is told, for instance, only perpetuates and strengthens the patriarchal and oppressive system.

I don't know how many times I've heard people say "I think it sucks that transgender people have so much discrimination just for being themselves", yet I've seen only a relatively small handful of heterosexual non-trans people (cisgender) who actually *do* anything about trying to change the system, to try to help abolish the discrimination. They will still be uncomfortable with trans people at the restaurant or the grocery store, or – *gasp!* – in their church or their apartment complex. I won't even touch the bathroom issue, you get the essence of what I'm saying.

I could elaborate on this and much more, but I'm saving the rest and more for another book, (or two or three!) I will conclude this subject with the following, which is another excerpt from Johnson's book (can you tell I liked it?) because I believe it defines the core belief system that has been instilled in each one of us from birth.

> When we gender what are inherently human qualities, we lock ourselves in a web of lies whose main consequence is to keep patriarchy going, for if society is to remain male dominated, male identified, and male centered, women and men must be seen as

fundamentally different so that men can control women as "other" (Johnson, 2007).

Only by seeking the truth, breaking out of the web of lies, can society begin to foster a new beginning where gender is no more relevant than what color of socks you are wearing today.

Epilogue

A Sharpened Pencil

"Be who you are and say what you feel, because those who mind don't matter, and those who matter don't mind." ~ *Bernard M. Baruch*

I AM LIKE other transgender people – I was born with a set of chromosomes that don't match up with who I really am. I was born an XX, and that will never change.

But through the years, through the struggles and the triumphs, there have been – oh, so many – changes and "edits" in life. I've rewritten the directions I've taken over and over, and will continue to do so until my time in this life is over. I'll continue to erase the mistakes, write in the good that I learned from them, and continue sharpening the pencil for as long as I can, because learning life is all about editing.

With that said; there is no end, just a future of new beginnings. Here is to a grand and conflict-free future for all transgender men, women and youth all over the world. I am proud to be part of the trans community. Hugs to you all. (Yes, I can hug – it's not just a "female" thing!)

###

Resources

There are many resources out there for transgender individuals as well as for our allies. A comprehensive listing of these resources can be found on the PFLAG's Transgender Support Network page which is listed below. I have listed only the resources I feel are important to providing some of the more crucial support in the lives and safety of transgender and gender non-conforming individuals.

Trans Lifeline
www.translifeline.com
(877) 565-8860

A hotline staffed by transgender people for transgender people. Trans Lifeline volunteers are ready to respond to whatever support needs members of our community might have. From their website: "Primarily for transgender people experiencing a crisis. This includes people who may be struggling with their gender identity and are not sure that they are transgender. While our goal is to prevent self-harm, we welcome the call of any transgender person in need. We will do our very best to connect them with services that can help them meet that need. If you are not sure whether you should call or not, then please call us."

The Trevor Project's 24/7 Lifeline
www.thetrevorproject.org
(866) 488-7386

The Trevor Project is the leading national organization providing crisis intervention and suicide prevention services to lesbian, gay, bisexual, transgender and questioning (LGBTQ) young people ages 13-24. TrevorChat is also available at http://www.thetrevorproject.org/pages/get-help-now#tc

TransYouth Family Allies
www.imatyfa.org
(8880 462-8932

TYFA empowers young people & their families through support, education, & outreach about gender identity & expression.

Transgender Law Center
www.transgenderlawcenter.org
(415) 865-0176

Transgender Law Center works to change law, policy, and attitudes so that all people can live safely, authentically, and free from discrimination regardless of their gender identity or expression. We envision a future where gender self-determination and authentic expression are seen as basic rights and matters of common human dignity.

PFLAG's Transgender Support Network
http://commnity.pflag.org/staff /transgender
(202) 467-8180

PFLAG is a resource for parents, families, and friends of people who are transgender and gender expansive. The resources on their pages will help advise you on how to better support a loved one as they move along their journey, and to help further your own understanding of your loved one's gender identity or expression.

Bibliography

Baldwin, J. (1984). *Notes of a native son* (Vol. 39). Beacon Press.

Bettcher, T. M. (2007). Evil Deceivers and Make-Believers: On Transphobic Violence and the Politics of Illusion. *Hypatia, 22*(3), 43-65.

Brett. (2012). Want to Feel Like a Man? Then Act Like One | The Art of Manliness http://www.artofmanliness.com/2012/05/13/want-to-feel-like-a-man-then-act-like-one/

Briere, J. & Elliot, D.M. (2003). Prevalence and psychological sequelae of self-reported childhood physical and sexual abuse in a general population sample of men and women. *Child Abuse & Neglect, 27*, 1205-1222.

Brown, M.E. (2015) The Truth About Campus Sexual Assaults. QuietMike.org. Retrieved from http://quietmike.org/2015/01/17/the-truth-about-campus-sexual-assaults/

Cook-Daniels, L. (2010). Thinking about the unthinkable: Transgender in an immutable binary world [Perspectives on Teaching]. *New Horizons in Adult Education and Human Resource Development, 24*(1), 63-70 Retrieved from http://files.eric.ed.gov/fulltext /EJ929952.pdf

Eliot, L. (2012). *Pink brain, blue brain: How small differences grow into troublesome gaps-and what we can do about it*. Oneworld Publications.

Franks, M. A. (2014). How to Feel Like a Woman, or Why Punishment Is a Drag. *UCLA Law Review*, *61*(3), 566-605.

Grace, C. (2015). The Triune Choice of Transgender Humans in a Binary World | Charissa's Grace Notes. Retrieved from http://charissagrace.com/2015/07/08/the-triune-choice-of-transgender-humans-in-a-binary-world/

Johnson, A.G. (2007). Where Are We? *The gender knot: Unraveling our patriarchal legacy.* Philadelphia, PA: Temple University Press. PDF

Jones, B. E., & Hill, M. J. (Eds.). (2008). *Mental health issues in lesbian, gay, bisexual, and transgender communities* (Vol. 21). American Psychiatric Pub.

Kidd, J. D., & Witten, T. M. (2007). Transgender and Trans sexual Identities: The Next Strange Fruit-Hate Crimes, Violence and Genocide Against the Global Trans-Communities. *Journal Of Hate Studies, 6*(1), 31-63.

Newsom, J.S. (2011). *Miss Representation* [Documentary]. USA: Girls Club Entertainment.

NGLTF and NCTE. (2009). Executive Summary: Injustice at every turn. *National Gay & Lesbian Task Force & National Center for Transgender Equality.* (PDF) Retrieved from http://endtransdiscrimination.org/report.html

Ray, N. (2006). Lesbian, Gay, Bisexual and Transgender Youth: An Epidemic of Homelessness, New York, NY: National Gay and Lesbian Task Force Policy

Institute and the National Coalition for the Homeless; Lambda Legal and Child Welfare League of America, 2012, LGBTQ Youth Risk Data, New York, NY: Lambda Legal, Washington, DC: Child Welfare League of America.

Statistics on Males and Eating Disorders | National Eating Disorders Association. (n.d.). Retrieved from https://www.nationaleatingdisorders.org/statistics-males-and-eating-disorders

Testa, R. J., Sciacca, L. M., Wang, F., Hendricks, M. L., Goldblum, P., Bradford, J., & Bongar, B. (2012). Effects of Violence on Transgender People. *Professional Psychology: Research & Practice, 43*(5), 452-459. doi:10.1037/a0029604

TLARS - TranScience Longitudinal Research Survey. Retrieved from http://www.transcience .org/

Trans Respect Versus Transphobia Worldwide. (2013). Retrieved from http://www.transrespect-transphobia.org/en/tvt-project/tmm-results/march-2013.htm

Veale J, Saewyc E, Frohard-Dourlent H, Dobson S, Clark B & the Canadian Trans Youth Health Survey Research Group (2015). Being Safe, Being Me: Results of the Canadian Trans Youth Health Survey. Vancouver, BC: Stigma and Resilience Among Vulnerable Youth Centre, School of Nursing, University of British Columbia. Retrieved from https://saravyc.sites.olt.ubc.ca/files/2015/05/

SARAVYC_Trans-Youth-Health-
Report_EN_Final_Web2.pdf

Wood, J. T. (2013). Ch. 1 The Study of Communication,
Gender and Culture. *Gendered lives: communication,
gender, and culture* (10th ed.,). Belmont, Calif.:
Cengage Learning

About the Author

Michael Eric Brown is the Founder and Executive Director of TransMentors International, Inc., a non-profit organization dedicated to supporting transgender men, women and youth in their day-to-day lives. You can visit the organization's website at http://www.transmentors.org.

As a student who is interested in how people's thoughts, feelings, and behaviors are influenced by the actual, imagined, or implied presence of others, Michael is working his way towards a PhD in Social Psychology in order to both educate society and provide research on the lives of transgender individuals.

As a professional freelance writer, he writes on a variety of subjects and engages his readers with his unique writing style. He is known for his contributions both on and offline, especially in the realm of social justice and gender concerns.

See Michael's current books at online retailers or on the Publisher's website at:

http://www.boundlessendeavors.com

Scheduled for release in 2016! Be sure to watch for

information about Michael's newest book with co-author Jackson Jantzen – unravelling the complex intersections of FTM gender transitions, lesbianism and feminism – *A Herstory of Transmasculine Identities.*

www.ingramcontent.com/pod-product-compliance
Lightning Source LLC
Chambersburg PA
CBHW062052270326
41931CB00013B/3040